BED AND BLESSINGS

ITALY

A Guide to Convents and Monasteries
Available for Overnight Lodging

June Walsh ■ Anne Walsh

Paulist Press

New York/Mahwah, New Jersey

Cover and interior design by Kokopelli Design Studio Inc.

Cover photo: The cloister walk of Hotel Il Christo, Verbania-Intra

Cover photo by Anne Walsh

Library of Congress Cataloging-in-Publication Data

Walsh, June.
    Bed and blessings:Italy/by June Walsh and Anne Walsh.
        p. cm.
    ISBN 0–8091–3848–4 (alk. paper)
    1. Monasteries—Guest accommodations—Italy—Directories.
I. Walsh, Anne. II. Title.
BX2622.W35   1999
647.9445—dc21   98-39727
                                                                CIP

Published by Paulist Press
997 Macarthur Boulevard
Mahwah, New Jersey 07430

www.paulistpress.com

Printed and bound in the United States of America

For Mike, Molly and Erin, with much gratitude and all our love.
Remember,

Semper progredi, nunquam regredi.

Acknowledgments

We owe a great deal of thanks to a number of people without whom our idea would never have become a book. Thank you for your many kindnesses.

Elena Bartoli
Randy Bass
Maria Booth
Paul Cardaci
Stephen Fields, S.J.
Barbara Fine
John Glavin
John Luria
Alan Mitchell
Katie Mondloch
Kathleen Mullen
Alida Pozzali
Jeffrey Shulman
Michelle Siemietkowski
Habte Teclemariam
Megan Tucker
Stephano Velotti
Jim Walsh, S.J.
Erin Walsh
Mike Walsh
Molly Walsh

And special thanks to our editor, Don Brophy.

CONTENTS

CONTENTS

INTRODUCTION

One does not come to Italy for niceness, one comes for life.

E. M. Forster
A Room with a View

Shaped by its people and patrons, friends and foes, Italy is always changing, forever evolving. And yet one constant, since the fourth century and the reign of Constantine, has been the presence of convents and monasteries. They are the natural outgrowth of the Catholic Church and a tangible expression of faith for millions in the world who call themselves Catholic. For centuries, the doors of these glorious buildings, some former palaces and villas, were closed to all but the men and women who had committed their lives to God. Today, with dwindling numbers of novices and rising costs of maintaining their religious houses, many nuns and monks, in an act of self-preservation and sheer brilliance, have opened their homes to the ecumenical public. For budget-wise and savvy travelers alike, this can mean paradise.

What, however, does *ecumenical* mean? What about those who are not Catholic? Most convents and monasteries in Italy, including all listed in this book, are open to everyone for short stays. Rest assured, visitors are not asked to show a baptismal certificate, just a passport, as all Italian hotels require. But for the uninitiated—or those who were not educated by the Madames of the Sacred Heart or raised with G. K. Chesterton's Father Brown mysteries—convent life in the late twentieth century can be likened to something between *The Sound of Music* and *Sister Act*: simplicity with an unspoken sense of worldliness.

Monastic rooms are normally spartan, breakfast is plain and there is sometimes a curfew to which residents must adhere. But staying in a religious guesthouse can offer affordable accommodations in the heart of some of Italy's finest cities and towns. Also at hand is the memorable experience of Italy as one of the world's centers of religion—religious affiliation, or lack thereof, aside. Indeed, it would be difficult not to notice that venturing behind the cloisters' mysterious walls begins a journey into another time, another place—in the real world, yet one step removed.

Bear in mind that these men and women are religious first, hoteliers second; they go about their daily routine—attending early morning mass, chanting and praying long before the sun has begun to rise. They must, however, support themselves, and as a result, no longer have the luxury of days past when they could truly retreat from the world. Today their faith and survival are intertwined, and guests to their homes benefit from an encounter as potentially intriguing as some of the monuments and museums they will explore during their visit.

To gather information for this book, we began our journey in Rome—a city full of wonder and fraught with frustrations. We had obtained from the Italian Tourist Agency in New York a list of more than one hundred convents offering hospitality in the Eternal City. On warm spring days we trekked from one side of the Tiber to the other. Some of the convents we visited are amazingly beautiful, rich in tradition and overwhelming in tranquility. Most are just steps from Italy's greatest attractions. The tour, however, also took its toll. The Tourist Agency's list was not up-to-date and featured many convents that do not offer hospitality, for which we spent many hours searching. We often pointed out the list to skeptical nuns who simply scowled, shook their heads and said, *"Errore, Errore!"* Interestingly, at the opposite end of the spectrum, we found that some of the dioceses of Italy are quite organized; many own and operate houses for retreatants and visitors, and they have employed the laity to assist them. Some of these establishments have even been designated "hotels" by the Italian tourist officials, despite the fact that they have chapels, crucifixes and other religious symbols on the premises. Welcome to Italy.

Over time, our odyssey continued to Italy's fabled hill towns, down to majestic seaside resorts, through rural villages and into vibrant and soulful cities where we had many a pleasant experience. In the pages that follow, you will read about many fascinating convents and monasteries. This is truly a unique way to travel, and as we discovered, one which offers a firsthand glimpse of the culture inherent in every Italian. This guide will serve as information for travelers who want to journey into Italy's history and culture without extravagant expense. And who knows—if you find yourself enjoying the virtues of convent lodgings, you might even make a habit of it.

DISCLAIMER

Every effort has been made to ensure the accuracy of all information contained herein. However, things change over time, and travelers should request updated information when making reservations. The publisher and authors cannot be responsible for errors or changes.

USEFUL INFORMATION

Making Reservations

Reservations should be made as far in advance as possible. The guesthouses tend to fill up rapidly, especially during the summer and holidays. We suggest that you telephone or fax for reservations. After making the reservation, send a personal check or credit card number with the dates of your visit to confirm your booking. We have a sample form for faxing or writing requests in Italian. Usually, the faxes are answered, but if not, send a deposit (by check) to hold your dates, and in most cases this will suffice.

Telephone Calls

To call Italy from the United States, dial 011 39 (the country code), and then add the city code and telephone number, making sure to include the 0 before the city code. For example, to dial Rome:

011-39-06-755-1234

Transportation Tips

CAR: Aside from using common sense, we discovered two things worth noting for those planning to rent a car.

A. Be aware that gasoline and toll roads are very expensive.

B. The red emergency boxes on the Autostrada should be used only in dire emergencies. These boxes will put you in touch with roadside assistance, but it is not free. In fact, it is quite time-consuming and extremely expensive.

TRAIN:

A. Purchase train tickets through a local travel agency and ALWAYS make a reservation (for a small fee), even if you are told it's not necessary. We had to stand from Venice to Florence on a crowded

Friday afternoon train because the tourist agency said a reservation was unnecessary!

B. Stamp the train ticket at the yellow boxes near the platform before boarding; otherwise you could receive a fine.

BUS:

A. Purchase tickets at local tobacco shops (usually near the bus stops).

B. Stamp the ticket in the yellow box once you board the bus; otherwise you could receive a fine.

CAMPANIA

A beautiful land of mountains, fertile fields and spectacular coastlines, Campania is a sizable region south of Rome and Lazio. Inhabited by one conqueror after another, the area finally settled into relative peace until World War II, when once again its lush green landscape ran red with the blood of battle. The capital, Naples, is a noisy, polluted, crowded and chaotic city set on the breathtaking Bay of Naples. It is home to a fine archaeological museum that houses many antiquities from the ruins of Pompeii and Herculaneum. These two cities were buried under volcanic ash when Mount Vesuvius erupted in A.D. 79 and were discovered nearly sixteen hundred years later in a fantastically preserved state.

The economy of the region depends largely upon tourists visiting these ruins as well as the chic resorts on the coast. Otherwise, the area has lower standards of living and education than the northern sections of Italy; the resulting crime and bureaucratic rigmarole inherent in the region does not make for easy living. Fortunately for visitors, these problems are miniscule in the resort areas. Most of the charming little towns on the coast are worthy of a visit; two of the most interesting have convents.

Capri is a lush, mountainous island in the Gulf of Naples known for its intoxicating beauty. The magnificent scenery and views are enhanced by the smells of lemon orchards, vineyards and olive groves. While there are no real beaches, the island has wonderful grottoes and caverns surrounded by the shimmering, blue Mediterranean. The lower town is a sophisticated, magical place of narrow streets, elegant boutiques and fun cafes and restaurants. For a touch of history and a glimpse into how the ancient rulers vacationed, the remains of Emperor Tiberius's villa are a fifty-minute walk from the town.

Ravello is a shining jewel along the Amalfi coastline. Located up a steep, winding road, the town offers relative peace and quiet from the hubbub of tourists who flock to the beaches during the summer. The little village has streets that are actually steps, a beautiful duomo, the Villa Rufolo, an eleventh-century delight, and the Villa Cimbrone, the gardens of which are not to be missed. Above all, Ravello offers a panorama of the cliffs and coast that is a joy at any time or any season.

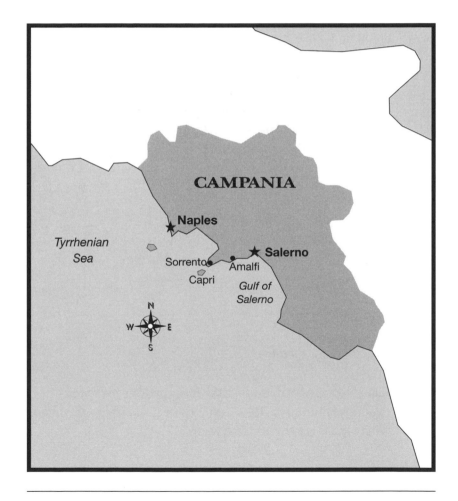

Capri

Villa Helios

Via Croce, 4

Capri 80073 (Napoli)

Tel. (081) 837 0240 ▪ Fax (081) 837 8060

Walking up a narrow road, at times no wider than six feet, one comes to the wrought iron gates of Villa Helios. A long, vine-covered canopy leads directly to the tiled entrance of this wonderful house. The bedrooms are plain and simple, but many offer spectacular views of the sea. A profusion of tropical trees and flowers fill the garden, which overlooks the Isle of Capri and the azure Mediterranean below. The villa is quite close to the festive town with its busy shops and restaurants and within easy walking distance of the ancient historic sites on the island.

Rooms: 20 singles, doubles and triples; all with bath.
Meals: Breakfast included; half board available upon request.
Price: 90.000L (single); 140.000L (double); 180.000L (triple).
Credit cards: Not accepted.
Curfew: Flexible.
Language(s) spoken: English.
Facilities: TV room.
Season: Open Easter–October.
DIRECTIONS:
Train station: Naples or Sorrento. Take ferry boat or hydrofoil (more expensive) to Capri. Take taxi, bus or funicular to the town center. Villa Helios is a five-minute walk.

Ravello

Casa Santa Chiara
Via Santa Chiara, 9
Ravello 84010 (Salerno)
Tel. (089) 857 145

High above the Amalfi coast in the charming village of Ravello is the Casa Santa Chiara. A climb of several stairs brings visitors to the entrance of this monastery, which provides spectacular views of the breathtaking Bay of Salerno from many of its rooms. The gracious nuns offer a tranquil retreat in a beautiful setting.

Rooms: 15 doubles and triples; half with bath.
Meals: None.
Price: 35.000L (without bath); 45.000L (with bath) per person.
Credit cards: Not accepted.
Curfew: No.
Language(s) spoken: Some English.
Facilities: Chapel.
Season: Open May–October.
DIRECTIONS:
Train station: Sorrento. Take a bus or ferry to Amalfi; then take a local bus to Piazza Vescovado in Ravello. The monastery is located at the top of a flight of stairs.

LAZIO

Lazio is a complex region of mountains, lakes, inland plains and coastal areas where inhabitants enjoy a standard of living above the national average. The population is largely centered in the area's capital city of Rome, where 55 percent of the residents dwell. The convents we discovered are all located in or just outside the Eternal City.

"Rome was not meant to move but to be beautiful," wrote Mark Helprin in *A Soldier of the Great War*. Rome is indeed beautiful, but Rome does nothing if not move; it is a cacophony of sights, sounds and smells that create a riotous buzz in this ancient city that is divided into a number of different neighborhoods, each with a distinct flavor and atmosphere. We were lucky to find some fantastic guesthouses in the following areas.

The historical center of Rome, also known as Centro Storico, is today the heart of the city; a labyrinth of narrow streets and wide piazzas, this area is home to some of Rome's finest baroque and classical architecture. A major sight is the Pantheon, Rome's best preserved monument, begun in 27 B.C. by Marcus Agrippa as a temple dedicated to the seven planetary gods, and rebuilt in A.D. 2 by the Emperor Hadrian. Located on the Piazza della Rotonda, this remarkable structure is naturally lit by a thirty-foot-wide opening at the top of the massive concrete dome. Here you will find the tombs of the famous painter Raphael and Victor Emanuel II, king of the first unified Italy.

Not an historic site, but one worth investigating in the same area is L'Eau Vive, a restaurant run by the International Missionary Sisters, located at 88 Via Monterone. Wonderful, simple Italian food is to be found here.

Close by, the central Roman square, Piazza Navona, is surrounded by baroque palaces and lively cafes. In the center of this spacious square, which was once used as a sports stadium, is Giovanni Lorenzo

Bernini's Fountain of the Four Rivers. Nearby, in the quiet Piazza Farnese, is one of Rome's most beautiful Renaissance palaces, the Palazzo Farnese, now the French Embassy, which Michelangelo helped to build.

To see another side of Rome, head for the Piazza di Spagna. From the Hassler to McDonald's, the neighborhood pulsates with the paradox of Rome: pricey, glitzy boutiques share the terrain with boisterous street vendors; elegantly attired shoppers stroll alongside exhausted, frazzled tourists; and sounds of Italian opera compete with boom box rock. At the center are the magnificent Spanish Steps, built in the early eighteenth century, which lead to the famous French church, Trinita dei Monti, and a small plaza from which to enjoy views of the city.

Another area with several convents is the triangle between the Colosseum, Saint Mary Maggiore and Saint John Lateran. Begun in A.D. 72, the Colosseum is now one of the most famous sites in Rome. Titus dedicated the monument in A.D. 80, sponsoring one hundred days of games in which nine thousand animals were slain in gladiatorial competitions. Today you can visit the structure's remains and view the exposed underground passages where the animals were held.

Churches in this area include Saint Mary Maggiore, which was founded in A.D. 432, and which is where you will find some exquisite art and architecture, along with the tomb of Bernini and Pope Sixtus V.

Nearby is Saint John the Lateran, once the papal residence and now the cathedral of Rome. Even today only the pope can celebrate mass in this grand church built in A.D. 314 by Constantine. It is located in the Piazza di Porta San Giovanni, where you will see the tallest and oldest (fifteenth-century B.C.) obelisk in Rome.

The few convents in the Aventine are actually situated on one of Rome's historic seven hills. Just beyond the Circus Maximus, the Tiber forms the western boundary of this elegant neighborhood of impressive homes, interesting churches and the municipal rose garden. Quieter than most of frenetic Rome, it is a delightful area in which to stay.

On the other side of the Tiber there are some wonderful guest-houses in Vatican City and Trastevere.

Vatican City, capital of the world's smallest independent state, is home to the pope and the center of Roman Catholicism. Set on 106 acres, it contains several places you will want to visit. The Vatican Gardens make up most of the Vatican See, covering sixty acres of lush lawns, wooded parkland and formal floral gardens.

Saint Peter's Basilica, built over the site of Saint Peter's grave, is the largest church in the world, offering standing room for one hundred thousand! Sights not to be missed are Michelangelo's *Pieta*, and Bernini's canopy, which covers the papal altar and the Tomb of the Fisherman. For an unforgettable view, go to the top of Michelangelo's Dome of Saint Peter's, nearly five hundred feet high.

The Sistine Chapel is lavishly decorated with frescoes depicting the life of Christ on the right, the life of Moses on the left and the Last Judgment on the wall behind the altar. The ceiling alone took Michelangelo four years to complete.

Between the Janiculum Hill and the Tiber, Trastevere has for centuries been a residential Roman neighborhood. In ancient Rome it was a port for traders from other Mediterranean countries. While the ships are long gone, the atmosphere of a waterfront area still exists in this colorful, densely populated quarter. To get a real flavor of Rome, visit the Trastevere Sunday Market.

NOTES

Rome

Casa Beata Margherita Caini
Via Fabio Massimo, 26
Rome 00192 (Roma)
Tel. (06) 324 2984 ▪ Fax (06) 324 2914

On a busy street in a residential and commercial section of Rome, the gracious sisters who own this casa offer large, plain rooms with recently remodeled baths. The atmosphere is calm and quiet. The location is excellent: close to the Vatican and within easy walking distance of Castel Sant'Angelo (the mausoleum Hadrian built for himself and his successors), the Tiber and many shops and restaurants in this vibrant part of the city.

Rooms: Singles, doubles and triples; all with bath, some with telephone.
Meals: Breakfast included.
Price: 50.000L (single); 75.000L (double); 100.000L (triple).
Credit cards: Not accepted.
Curfew: 10:00 P.M.
Language(s) spoken: No English.
Facilities: Elevator, chapel.
Season: Open all year.
DIRECTIONS:
Train station: Termini. Take metro A to Ottaviano/S. Pietro.

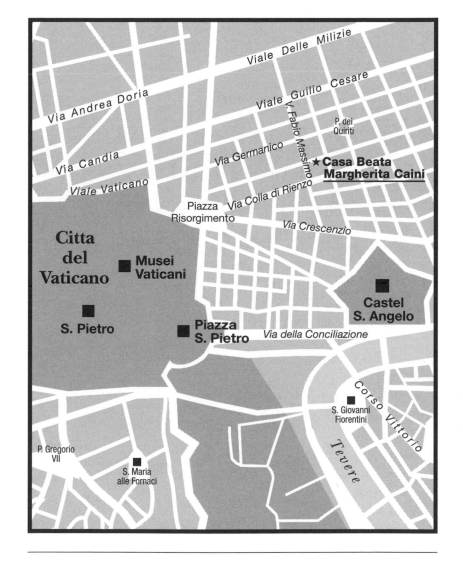

Casa di Santa Brigida

Piazza Farnese, 96

Rome 00185 (Roma)

Tel. (06) 688 9259 ▪ Fax (06) 688 91573

Located in the quiet Piazza Farnese, the Casa di Santa Brigida stands across from one of Rome's most beautiful Renaissance palaces, the Palazzo Farnese, now the French Embassy, which Michelangelo helped build. Walking into the grand foyer of this ancient convent, where its namesake, Saint Birgitta of Sweden, lived until her death in 1373, our eyes fell upon a pile of Louis Vuitton luggage—an early indication that the prices are higher here than those of most guesthouses. On the ground floor, fresh flowers grace reception rooms furnished with old leather couches and chairs. Floors are covered with large, lovely Oriental rugs. Upstairs are a small library, a roof terrace, a chapel and several sitting rooms. The sisters here are, unfortunately, often less than gracious, so make sure you really want to stay here before spending the same price you could pay at a nearby hotel.

Rooms: 24 singles and doubles; all with bath and telephone.
Meals: Breakfast included; half and full board available upon request.
Price: 145.000L (single); 250.000L (double).
Credit cards: Not accepted.
Curfew: None.
Language(s) spoken: English, French.
Facilities: Elevator, TV room, meeting room, library, chapel.
Season: Open all year.
DIRECTIONS:
Train station: Termini. Take bus no. 64 to Corso V. Emanuele II.

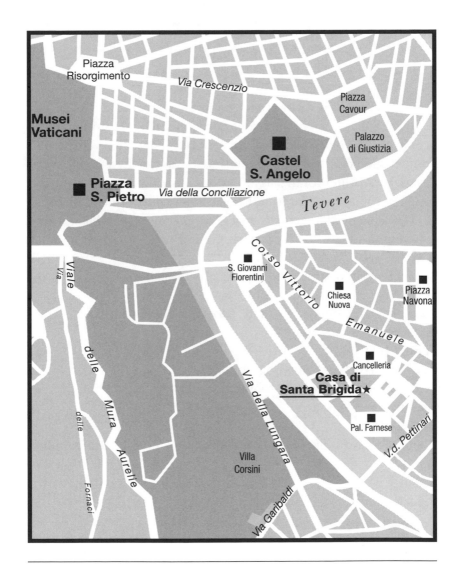

Casa di Santa Francesca Romana

Via dei Vascellari, 61

Rome 00153 (Roma)

Tel. (06) 581 2125 ▪ Fax (06) 588 2408

In the early 1400s, Saint Francesca Romana lived and died in this house. She had spent the better part of her life ministering to the people of her neighborhood, Trastevere. Today, her refurbished home is offered to tourists and pilgrims for hospitality and still serves as a spiritual center for the area. The accommodations are good, the common rooms quite large and a nice inner courtyard is available to all. This ancient Roman quarter of grimy, narrow streets has become quite trendy of late and is filled with popular shops and restaurants.

Rooms: Singles, doubles and triples; all with bath.
Meals: None.
Price: 80.000L (single); 116.000L (double); 126.000L (triple).
Credit cards: Not accepted.
Curfew: 1:00 A.M.
Language(s) spoken: Some English.
Facilities: Elevator, meeting rooms, chapel.
Season: Open all year.
DIRECTIONS:
Train station: Termini. Take bus no. 75 or no. 170 to Piazza Sonnino.

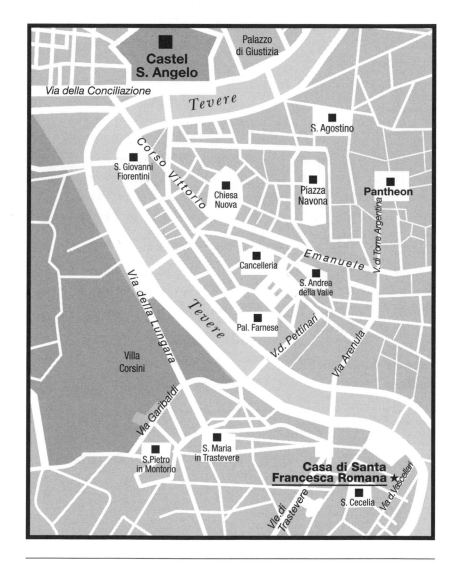

Casa Domitilla
Via delle Sette Chiese, 280
Rome 00147 (Roma)
Tel. (06) 513 3956 ▪ Fax (06) 513 5461

Out near the ancient Appian Way and the famous Catacombs of San Calisto and San Sebastian, Casa Domitilla provides comfort and convenience for the busy traveler. The rooms in this modern brick building are pleasant, and all are equipped with telephones, modern baths and excellent reading lights—which are a rarity in Europe. The dining room is spacious and airy, and a bar, TV room and lovely park are available for guests. The nearby bus line has excellent service to all of Rome.

Rooms: Singles and doubles; all with bath and telephone.
Meals: Breakfast extra (12.000L); half board available upon request.
Price: 77.000L (single); 106.000L (double).
Credit cards: Not accepted.
Curfew: Flexible.
Language(s) spoken: English.
Facilities: Parking, elevator, TV room, meeting room, restaurant, bar, chapel.
Season: Open all year.
DIRECTIONS:
Train station: Termini. Take bus no. 613 or no. 714 to Piazza Navigatori.

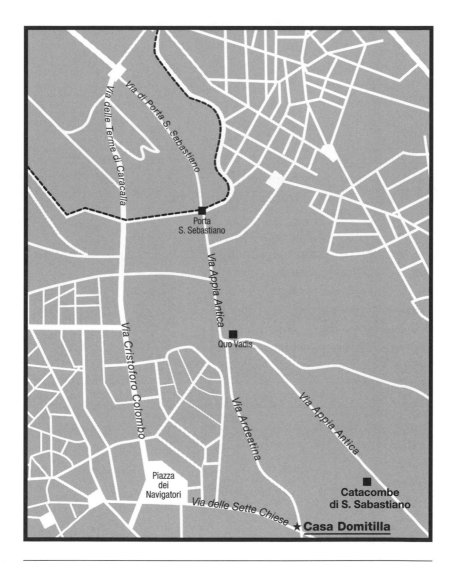

Casa Famiglia Suore
Benedettine di Carita
Via di Torre Argentina, 76
Rome 00186 (Roma)
Tel. (06) 688 05091

This Benedictine pensione is primarily for female students, but the sisters will accept women travelers if they have space available. Safe, clean and very modest, this convent is located in a large, drab building just steps away from the Pantheon, Il Gesu (the spectacular church where Saint Ignatius of Loyola is buried) and many other sites, shops and cafes of historic Rome.

Rooms: 23 singles for women only; none with bath.
Meals: Full board only.
Price: 45.000L per person.
Credit cards: Not accepted.
Curfew: 10:30 P.M.
Language(s) spoken: No English.
Facilities: Elevator, meeting room, salon.
Season: Open all year.
DIRECTIONS:
Train station: Termini. Take bus no. 64 to Largo Torre Argentina.

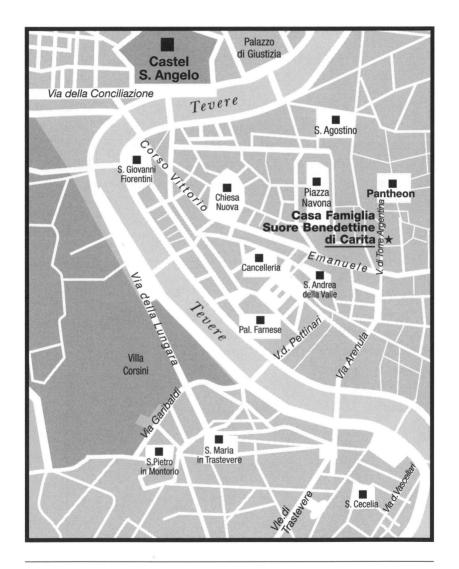

Palazzo
di Giustizia

**Castel
S. Angelo**

Via della Conciliazione

Tevere

S. Agostino

Corso Vittorio

S. Giovanni
Fiorentini

Chiesa
Nuova

Piazza
Navona

Pantheon

**Casa Famiglia
Suore Benedettine
di Carita** ★

V. di Torre Argentina

Emanuele

Cancelleria

S. Andrea
della Valle

Via della Lungara

Tevere

Pal. Farnese

V.d. Pettinari

Via Arenula

Villa
Corsini

Via Garibaldi

S.Pietro
in Montorio

S. Maria
in Trastevere

Vle.di Trastevere

S. Cecelia

Via d.Vascellari

Casa Il Rosario
Via Sant'Agata dei Goti, 10
Rome 00184 (Roma)
Tel. (06) 679 2346 ■ Fax (06) 699 41106

C lose to the Colosseum and ruins of ancient Rome, Casa Rosario sits in a very old and modest part of the city. The sisters are especially hospitable and pleasant; they have recently updated all the rooms, which are simple, clean and comfortable. A special feature of this house is the rooftop garden, which is a fairly unusual amenity in this thriving metropolis.

Rooms: Singles, doubles and triples; all with bath.
Meals: Breakfast included.
Price: 60.000L per person.
Credit cards: Not accepted.
Curfew: 11:15 P.M.
Language(s) spoken: Some English.
Facilities: Elevator, TV room, chapel.
Season: Open all year.
DIRECTIONS:
Train station: Termini. Take bus no. 64 to Via Nazionale.

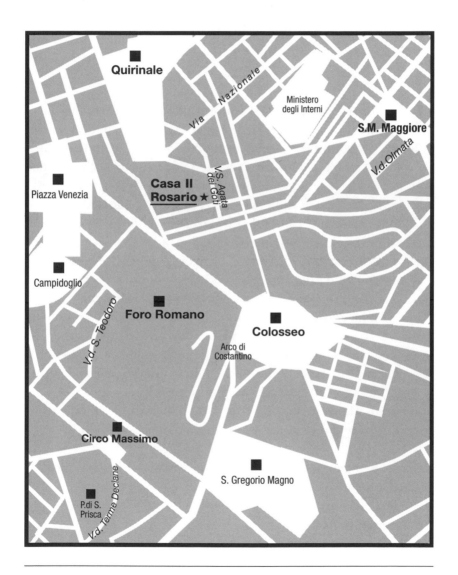

Quirinale

Via Nazionale

Ministero
degli Interni

S.M. Maggiore

V.d.Olmata

Piazza Venezia

Casa II
Rosario ★

V.S. Agata
dei Goti

Campidoglio

V.d. S. Teodoro

Foro Romano

Colosseo

Arco di
Costantino

Circo Massimo

S. Gregorio Magno

P.di S.
Prisca

V.d. Terme Deciane

Casa Kolbe
Via San Teodoro, 44
Rome 00186 (Roma)
Tel. (06) 679 4974 ▪ Fax (06) 699 41550

At Auschwitz in July 1941, ten prisoners were selected to die of starvation as punishment for the escape of three prisoners. Franciszek Gajowniczek begged for his life so that he could be reunited with his family. A Franciscan named Maximilian Kolbe stepped forward saying, "I am a Catholic priest. I wish to die for that man. I am old; he has a wife and children." The Nazi commander agreed and Kolbe was sent to an underground cell where he went without food for two weeks and was ultimately killed by lethal injection administered by the camp doctor. In 1972 Gajowniczek, who was reunited with his family after the war, expressed his gratitude for Kolbe's enormous sacrifice. Ten years later, Father Kolbe was canonized a saint.

Today an enormous monastery named for Maximilian Kolbe is a house of hospitality. The public rooms are unimaginative, the upstairs hallways long and dim, and the bedrooms stark. The Casa's best attribute is the location—adjacent to the Forum and within walking distance of many ruins of ancient Rome—the Colosseum and Circus Maximus, among others. The management will recommend a marvelous restaurant around the corner.

Rooms: 65 singles, doubles, triples; all with bath and telephone.
Meals: None.
Price: 90.000L (single); 120.000 (double); 150.000 (triple).
Credit cards: All major.
Curfew: Flexible.

Language(s) spoken: English.
Facilities: Parking, elevator, TV room, restaurant, bar, chapel.
Season: Open all year.
DIRECTIONS:
Train station: Termini. Take a taxi.

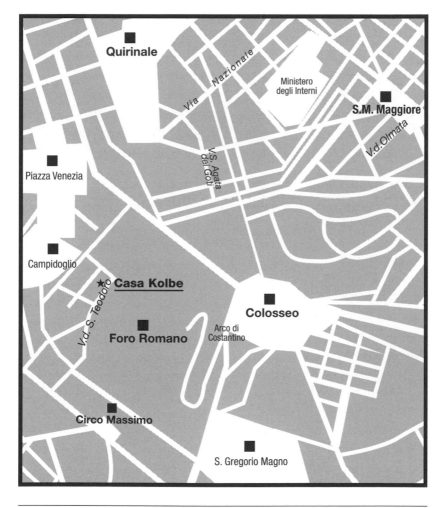

Casa Mater Ecclesiae
Salita di Monte del Gallo, 25-A
Rome 00165 (Roma)
Tel. (06) 637 4653

Located on a quiet street up the hill from the Vatican, this is an unpretentious, modern and well-run guesthouse. All of the rooms are of good size and many have balconies; to see Saint Peter's Basilica from "your room," ask for accommodations with a view on the second or third floor. Proximity to the bus line makes it convenient for visiting all parts of Rome.

Rooms: Singles, doubles and triples; all with bath.
Meals: Breakfast included; full board available upon request except Sundays and holidays.
Price: 65.000L (single) 92.000L (double); 138.000L (triple).
Credit cards: Not accepted.
Curfew: 11:00 P.M.
Language(s) spoken: No English.
Facilities: Elevator, chapel.
Season: Open all year.
DIRECTIONS:
Train station: Termini. Take bus no. 64 to Vio S. Pio X and transfer to bus no. 34, which travels along Via Monte del Gallo (Salita di Monte del Gallo is a side street).

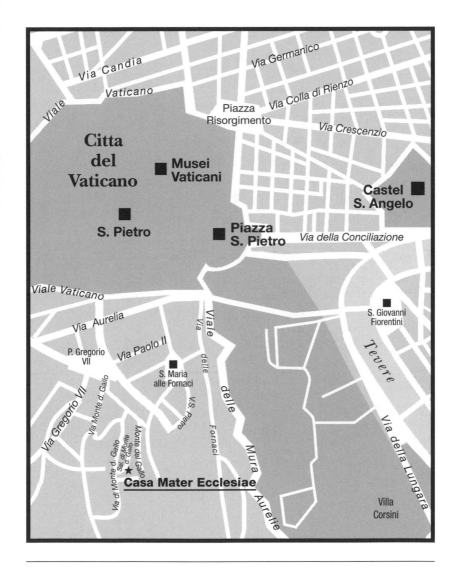

Casa Mater Immaculata
Via Monte del Gallo, 38
Rome 00165 (Roma)
Tel. (06) 630 863

G uests to Casa Mater Immaculata can find peace and relaxation in the large, beautiful garden of this Italian villa nestled in the hills above Saint Peter's Square. Adjacent to the garden is a delightful room with wicker tables and chairs; a pretty dining room where guests take breakfast is close by. Recently remodeled bedrooms and baths add to the comfort of this casa. Situated in a good residential area, it is within walking distance of a bus stop.

Rooms: 24 singles and doubles; all with bath (some located outside room).
Meals: Breakfast included.
Price: 45.000L–62.000L (single); 53.000L–70.000L (double).
Credit cards: Not accepted.
Curfew: Flexible.
Language(s) spoken: French, some German, Spanish.
Facilities: Chapel.
Season: Open all year except January.
DIRECTIONS:
Train station: Termini. Take bus no. 64 to Vio S. Pio X and transfer to bus no. 34, which travels along Via Monte del Gallo.

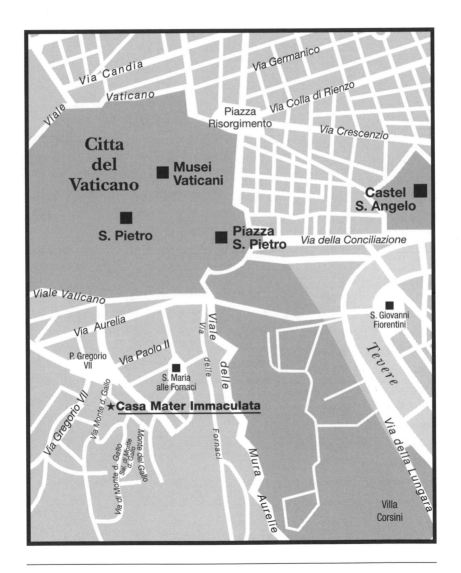

Casa Nostra Signora dell'Atonement
Via Monte del Gallo, 105
Rome 00165 (Roma)
Tel. (06) 630 782 ▪ Fax (06) 638 6149

A ten-minute walk up the hill from Saint Peter's Square brings travelers to this convent of Franciscan nuns whose mother-house is in New York. The sizable cream stucco house offers many conveniences for guests: a peaceful garden terrace, a TV room and a library filled with information about Rome. The sisters have also installed vending machines for snacks, added a washer and dryer, and for a small fee, they will do your ironing! The rooms are plain, but their balconies have terrific views. The hospitality is warm and gracious and the house is efficiently managed.

Rooms: 20 singles, doubles and triples; all with bath.
Meals: Breakfast included; half and full board available upon request.
Price: 55.000L (single); 90.000L (double); 135.000L (triple).
Credit cards: Not accepted.
Curfew: 11:00 P.M.
Language(s) spoken: English.
Facilities: Parking, elevator, TV room, meeting room, laundry, vending machines, chapel.
Season: Open all year except December 22–January 7.
DIRECTIONS:
Train station: Termini. Take bus no. 64 to Vio S. Pio X and transfer to bus no. 34, which travels along Via Monte del Gallo.

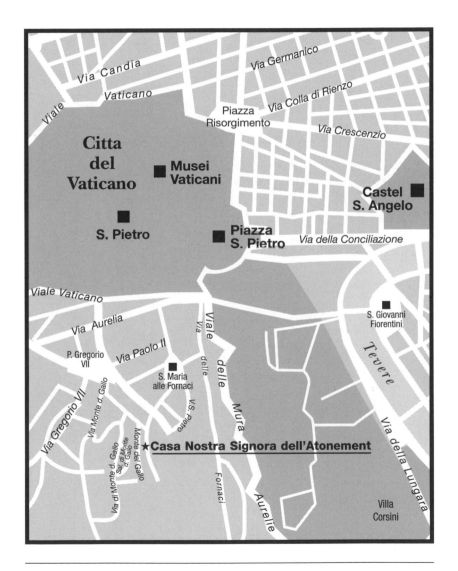

Casa Paolo VI
Viale Vaticano, 92
Rome 00165 (Roma)
Tel. (06) 397 23797 ▪ Fax (06) 397 23792

In view of the formidable, ancient, gray walls of Vatican City, this pretty casa offers a peaceful respite from the hubbub of Rome. Orange and lemon trees flank the cobblestone courtyard in front of the beige stone house. The interior reception rooms were filled with antiques and flowers when we visited, but the accommodations were being remodeled. The house is scheduled to reopen in September 1998. The magnificent Vatican museums and gardens are just steps away from the house, and many "tourist" restaurants and shops are down the street.

Rooms: 25 singles; none with bath.
Meals: Breakfast included.
Price: 35.000L per person.
Credit cards: Not accepted.
Curfew: None.
Language(s) spoken: No English.
Facilities: Elevator, chapel.
Season: Open all year.
DIRECTIONS:
Train station: Termini. Take metro A to Ottaviano/San Pietro and head toward Saint Peter's. Viale Vaticano is a long walk uphill (take taxi with luggage). Casa Paolo is on the right.

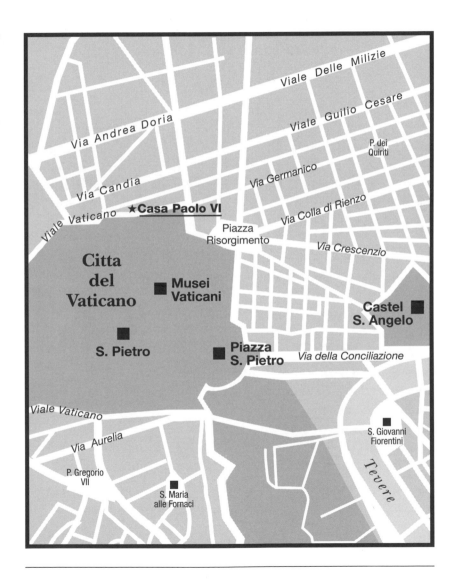

Viale Delle Milizie

Viale Guilio Cesare

Via Andrea Doria

P. dei Quiriti

Via Candia

Via Germanico

Viale Vaticano

★**Casa Paolo VI**

Via Colla di Rienzo

Piazza Risorgimento

Via Crescenzio

Citta del Vaticano

Musei Vaticani

Castel S. Angelo

S. Pietro

Piazza S. Pietro

Via della Conciliazione

Viale Vaticano

Via Aurelia

S. Giovanni Fiorentini

Tevere

P. Gregorio VII

S. Maria alle Fornaci

Casa per Ferie Madre Maria Eugenia
Viale Romania, 32
Rome 00197 (Roma)
Tel. (06) 844 82300 ▪ Fax (06) 844 82302

C asa per Ferie Madre Maria Eugenia is set in a large parklike setting with a security guard at the entrance. The lovely grounds,
landscaped with flowers, shrubs and grand trees, are a perfect place
for summer picnics. A kindergarten is on the premises, as evidenced
by the play equipment. The accommodations are clean and comfortable; some open on to a large terrace. Public transportation and
a few restaurants are nearby.

Rooms: 58 singles, doubles and triples; all with bath and telephone.
Meals: Breakfast extra (3.000L); full board and picnics available
upon request.
Price: 60.000L (single); 90.000L (double); 120.000L (triple).
Credit cards: Not accepted.
Curfew: None.
Language(s) spoken: Some English.
Facilities: Parking, elevator, meeting rooms, vending machines, chapel.
Season: Open all year.
DIRECTIONS:
Train station: Termini. Take bus no. 4 to Viale Romania.

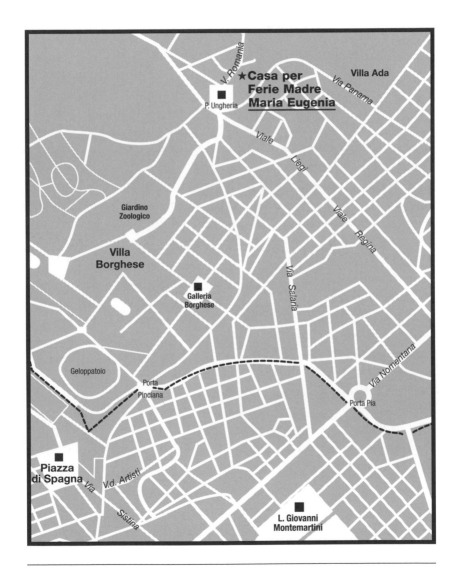

★**Casa per Ferie Madre Maria Eugenia**

Villa Ada

Via Romania

Via Panama

P. Ungheria

Viale Liegi

Via Regina

Giardino Zoologico

Villa Borghese

Galleria Borghese

Via Salaria

Geloppatoio

Via Nomentana

Porta Pinciana

Porta Pia

Piazza di Spagna

V.d. Artisti

Via

Sistina

L. Giovanni Montemartini

Casa per Ferie S. Maria alle Fornaci

Piazza S. Maria alle Fornaci, 27

Rome 00165 (Roma)

Tel. (06) 393 67632 ▪ Fax (06) 393 66795

Founded in 1198 by a Parisian, Saint John de Matha, to offer the option of humanitarian service in place of military service, the Order of Trinitarians have been offering hospitality throughout Europe and the Middle East since the thirteenth century. Today, their home is situated on a lively piazza just a short walk to the Vatican. The public rooms are very lovely with marble used extensively. The bedrooms are simple and comfortable. Restaurants, shops and good transportation are close by.

Rooms: Singles, doubles and triples; all with bath and telephone.
Meals: Breakfast included.
Price: 90.000L (single); 120.000L (double); 135.000L (triple).
Credit cards: Not accepted.
Curfew: 11:00 P.M.
Language(s) spoken: English.
Facilities: Elevator, TV room, meeting rooms, chapel.
Season: Open all year.
DIRECTIONS:
Train station: Termini. Take bus no. 64 to Piazza Venezia and transfer to bus no. 62.

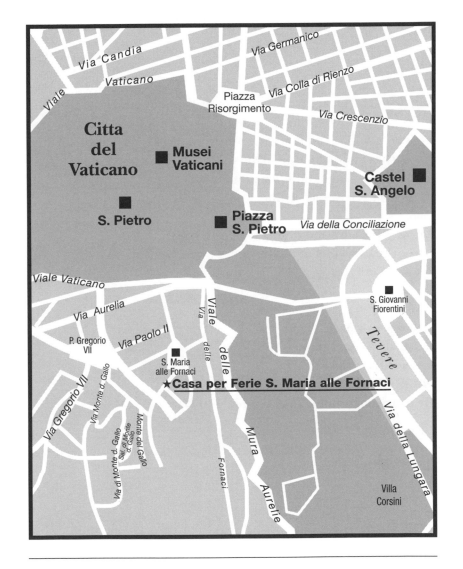

Casa per Ferie San Giuseppe
Via Iberia, 27
Rome 00183 (Roma)
Tel. (06) 704 91482 ▪ Fax (06) 772 06535

Situated in a marginal area of Rome, this very pretty Italian villa is run by gracious Franciscan sisters. The accommodations are perfectly acceptable, and there is a courtyard planted with colorful flowers, bushes and palm trees. Due to the neighborhood, however, we would not recommend it for women traveling alone; for couples or small groups it would be fine.

Rooms: 21 singles and doubles; all with bath.
Meals: Breakfast included; full board available upon request.
Price: 45.000L (single); 80.000L (double).
Credit cards: Not accepted.
Curfew: 11:00 P.M.
Language(s) spoken: No English.
Facilities: Parking, chapel.
Season: Open all year.
DIRECTIONS:
Train station: Termini. Take bus no. 4 to Piazza Tuscolo.

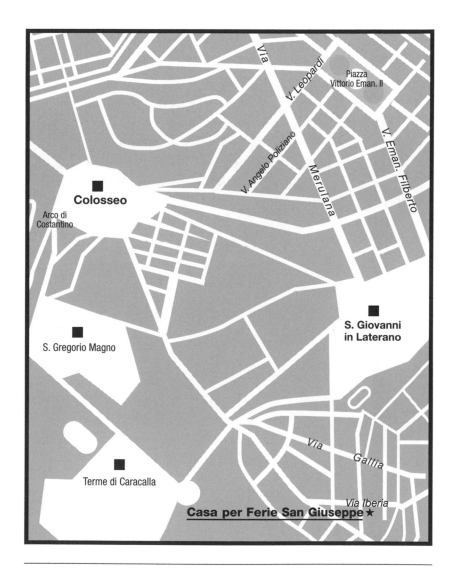

Casa Soggiorno Sant'Elisabetta
Via dell'Olmata, 9
Rome 00184 (Roma)
Tel. (06) 488 5229 ▪ Fax (06) 488 4066

A pretty statue of Saint Elizabeth sits in a niche above the threshold of this wonderful terra-cotta-colored convent. Completely renovated three years ago, the interior is quite modern and comfortable. A pretty chapel and a delightful oasis of flowers, shrubs and palm trees situated behind the house are some of the highlights found here. The sisters are very gracious and the location is excellent—close to all forms of public transportation and within walking distance of the train station.

Rooms: 35 singles, doubles and triples; all with bath.
Meals: Breakfast included.
Price: 55.000L (single); 97.000L (double); 122.000L (triple).
Credit cards: Not accepted.
Curfew: None.
Language(s) spoken: English, German.
Facilities: Elevator, chapel.
Season: Open all year.
DIRECTIONS:
Train station: Termini. Take bus no. 714 to Piazza S. Maria Maggiore, or walk the six blocks from the station.

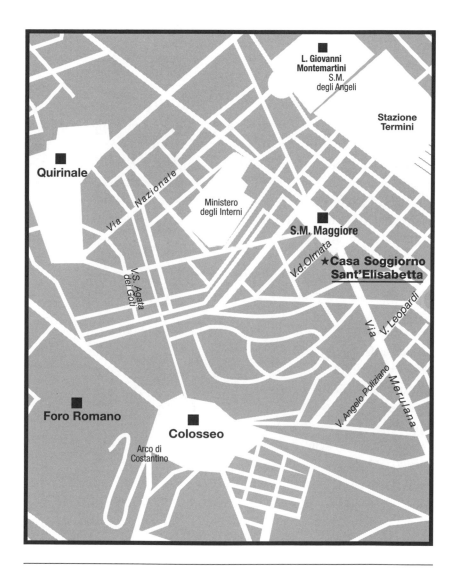

L. Giovanni
Montemartini
S.M.
degli Angeli

Stazione
Termini

Quirinale

Via Nazionale

Ministero
degli Interni

S.M. Maggiore

V.d.Olmata

★Casa Soggiorno
Sant'Elisabetta

V.S. Agata
dei Goti

Via V. Leopardi

V. Angelo Poliziano

Merulana

Foro Romano

Colosseo

Arco di
Costantino

Casa Tra Noi
Via Monte del Gallo, 113
Rome 00165 (Roma)
Tel. (06) 393 87355 ▪ Fax (06) 393 87446

Located on a steep hill on the south side of the Vatican, Casa Tra Noi is a multistory peach-colored building offering hospitality to pilgrims and tourists alike. Nice, comfortable bedrooms open on to balconies generously decorated with potted flowers. Guests are invited to relax in the bright, airy common rooms or on the large terrace. Efficient management of this guesthouse, where a bar and snack machines have been added for visitors' convenience, provides a comfortable atmosphere.

Rooms: Singles, doubles and triples; all with bath and telephone.
Meals: Breakfast included; half and full board available upon request.
Price: 82.000L (single); 142.000L (double); 207.000L (triple).
Credit cards: Not accepted.
Curfew: Flexible.
Language(s) spoken: English.
Facilities: Parking, elevator, TV room, meeting room, restaurant, bar, chapel.
Season: Open all year.
DIRECTIONS:
Train station: Termini. Take bus no. 64 to Vio S. Pio X and then transfer to bus no. 34, which travels along Via Monte del Gallo.

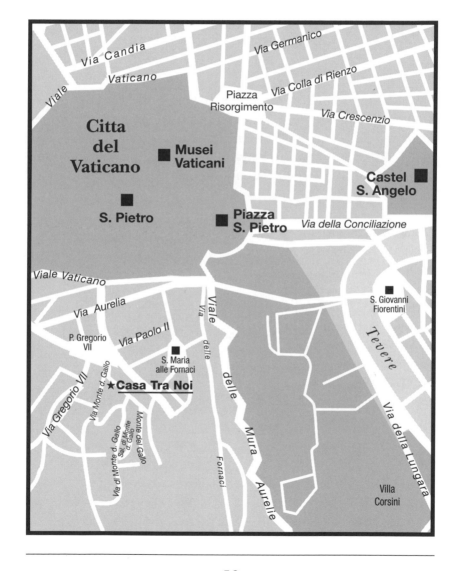

Casa Unione Mysterium Christi
Via Merulana, 174
Rome 00185 (Roma)
Tel. (06) 704 92421/759 2421

At their guesthouse, located on a wide, busy, tree-lined street, the Suore di Cristo (Sisters of Christ) welcome all visitors. Small and plain, this convent offers modern accommodations and good food. Close to the bus line and metro, the house is also within walking distance of the Colosseum, Roman Forum and fun shops and cafes.

Rooms: Singles and doubles; all with bath.
Meals: Half board only.
Price: 70.000L.
Credit cards: Not accepted.
Curfew: 10:30 P.M.
Language(s) spoken: No English.
Facilities: Elevator, chapel.
Season: Open all year.
DIRECTIONS:
Train station: Termini. Take bus no. 714, which travels along Via Merulana.

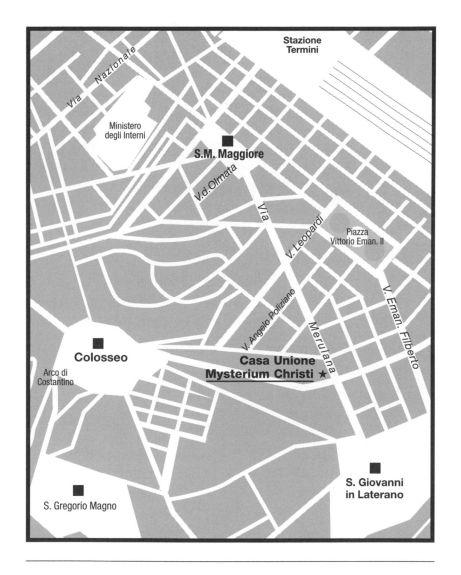

Stazione Termini

Via Nazionale

Ministero degli Interni

S.M. Maggiore

V.d.Olmata

Via

V. Leopardi

Piazza Vittorio Eman. II

V. Angelo Poliziano

V. Eman. Filberto

Merulana

Colosseo

Arco di Costantino

Casa Unione Mysterium Christi ★

S. Giovanni in Laterano

S. Gregorio Magno

Convento San Francesco

Via Nicolo V, 35

Rome 00165 (Roma)

Tel. (06) 393 66531

Directed by Franciscan sisters from Syracuse, New York, this stone guesthouse is a short walk up the hill from Saint Peter's Square. The convent's desirable location near the entrance to the magnificent Vatican Gardens and its close proximity to a bus line provide convenience for travelers. The public and private rooms are simple and comfortable, and there is a roof terrace where guests can relax and enjoy the view of the great basilica.

Rooms: 16 singles and doubles; none with bath.
Meals: Breakfast included; half board available upon request.
Price: 50.000L per person.
Credit cards: Not accepted.
Curfew: Flexible.
Language(s) spoken: English.
Facilities: Elevator, chapel.
Season: Open all year.
DIRECTIONS:
Train station: Termini. Take bus no. 64 to Piazza Venezia and then transfer to bus no. 46, which stops near Via Nicolo V.

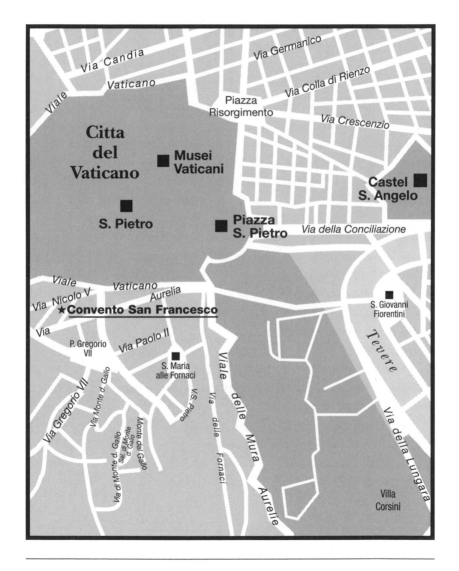

Eremo Domenicane di Santa Rosa
Via del Pescaccio, 101
Rome 00166 (Roma)
Tel. (06) 661 82247 ▪ Fax (06) 661 82804

Closer to the airport than to downtown Rome, the Dominican Sisters of Saint Rose offer gracious hospitality in a very peaceful setting. The grounds are extensive, planted with pine trees, shrubs and flowers. The stone and brick buildings are rather utilitarian, but the public rooms are bright, airy and user-friendly. The accommodations are fine, and some rooms offer balconies.

Rooms: Singles, doubles and triples; all with bath.
Meals: Breakfast included; half and full board available upon request.
Price: 85.000L (single); 130.000L (double); 195.000L (triple); plus one-time 4.000L charge.
Credit cards: Not accepted.
Curfew: None.
Language(s) spoken: No English.
Facilities: Parking, elevator, TV room, meeting rooms, bar, chapel.
Season: Open all year.
DIRECTIONS:
Airport: Leonardo da Vinci (Fiumicino).
Car: Take the Autostrada toward Rome; at "Uscita 30," head north to "Uscita 33," Pescaccio, and bear to the right.

Fraterna Domus
Via Mont Brianzo, 62
Rome 00186 (Roma)
Tel. (06) 688 02727 ■ Fax (06) 683 2691

Situated close to the Tiber in the heart of old Rome, Fraterna Domus is a dream location for walkers. The Vatican, Piazza Navona, Pantheon, Trastevere, Spanish Steps and most of the ancient city can be visited without ever using a vehicle. The bedrooms are more than adequate, beamed ceilings create a cozy atmosphere in the dining room, and there is a flower-filled rooftop terrace where guests can enjoy relaxing moments and a different view of Italy's capital. The sisters are delightful and very helpful.

Rooms: Singles and doubles; all with bath.
Meals: Breakfast included; half and full board available upon request.
Price: 70.000L (single); 100.000L (double).
Credit cards: Not accepted.
Curfew: 11:00 P.M.
Language(s) spoken: Some English.
Facilities: Chapel.
Season: Open all year.
DIRECTIONS:
Train station: Termini. Take bus no. 70.

Hotel Domus Aventina

Via di Santa Prisca, 11B

Rome 00153 (Roma)

Tel. (06) 574 6135 ▪ Fax (06) 573 00044

Overlooking the cloister of the church of Saint Prisca (built above a home where Saint Peter stayed) are the tasteful, well-appointed rooms of this three-star hotel. An unpretentious lobby leads to a large terrace encircled by orange groves and an enviable rose garden. Set on the Aventine Hill, one of Rome's seven hills and the site where Remus was slain, it is a peaceful and quiet haven within easy reach of the Colosseum, Forum, Circus Maximus and all of ancient Rome.

Rooms: Singles and doubles; all with bath, telephone, TV and safe.
Meals: Breakfast included.
Price: 190.000L (single); 290.000L (double).
Credit cards: All major accepted.
Curfew: None.
Language(s) spoken: English.
Facilities: Parking, air-conditioning, chapel.
Season: Open all year.
DIRECTIONS:
Train station: Termini. Take metro B to Circo Massimo.

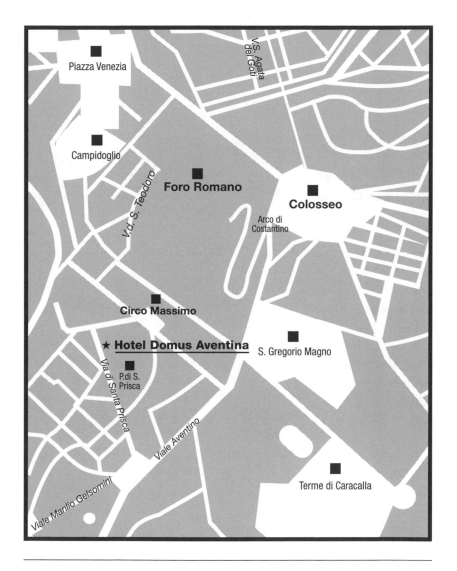

Piazza Venezia

V. S. Agata dei Goti

Campidoglio

V.d. S. Teodoro

Foro Romano

Colosseo

Arco di Costantino

Circo Massimo

★ Hotel Domus Aventina

S. Gregorio Magno

Via di Santa Prisca

P.di S. Prisca

Viale Aventino

Viale Manlio Gelsomini

Terme di Caracalla

Hotel Santa Prisca

Largo Gelsomini, 25

Rome 00153 (Roma)

Tel. (06) 574 1917 ▪ Fax (06) 574 6658

Surrounded by its own park in the elegant Aventine section of Rome, Hotel Santa Prisca offers a warm welcome to travelers. Between the sisters' house and the hotel is a lovely courtyard with a wishing well. On another side of the building there is a large flowered terrace—a wonderful place to relax. The public rooms and accommodations are modern and pleasant. To avoid traffic noise we recommend asking for an inside room.

Rooms: 50 singles and doubles; all with bath, telephone and TV.
Meals: Breakfast extra (12.000L).
Price: 145.000L (single); 175.000L (double).
Credit cards: All major.
Curfew: None.
Language(s) spoken: English.
Facilities: Parking, elevator, meeting room, restaurant, bar, chapel.
Season: Open all year.
DIRECTIONS:
Train Station: Termini. Take metro B to Piramide or bus no. 27.

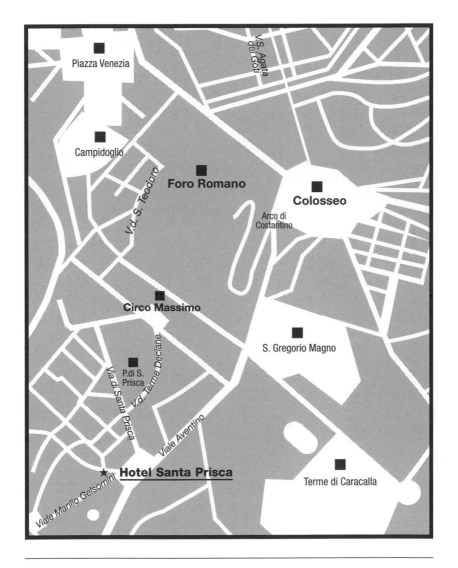

Hotel Siso V
Via dei Pettinari, 64
Rome 00186 (Roma)
Tel. (06) 686 8843 ▪ Fax (06) 683 088 22

Owned by the Pallottine Order, this hotel is currently undergoing extensive renovations. Brochures and prices should be ready in late 1998, with a scheduled opening in early 1999. The location is unbeatable: near Il Gesu, Pantheon, Campo dei Fiori and the shops, cafes and restaurants of "Centro Storico."

DIRECTIONS:
Train station: Termini. Take bus no. 65 to Ponte Sisto.

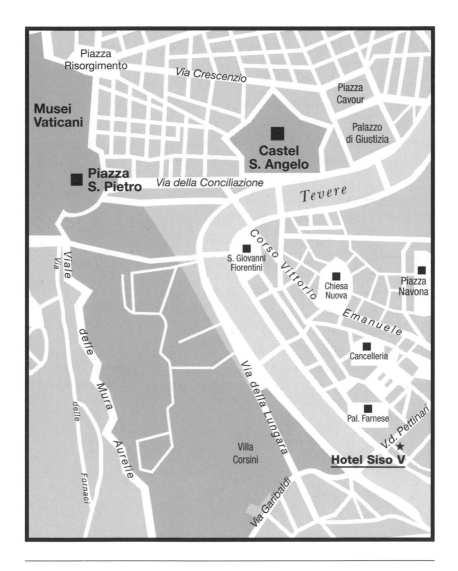

Istituto Eugenia Ravasco
Via Stazione di S. Pietro, 37
Rome 00165 (Roma)
Tel. (06) 393 66094 ■ Fax (06) 393 66094

In the summertime this university pensione is opened to visitors. The simple accommodations are clean and comfortable. The location is wonderful: close to public transportation and within walking distance of the Vatican, shops and restaurants.

Rooms: Singles and doubles; all with bath.
Meals: Breakfast included; half and full board available upon request.
Price: 55.000L (single); 100.000L (double).
Credit cards: Not accepted.
Curfew: Flexible.
Language(s) spoken: No English.
Facilities: Elevator, chapel.
Season: Open June–August.
DIRECTIONS:
Train station: Termini. Take bus no. 64 to Largo Argentina and then transfer to bus no. 62. Get off at the last stop before the terminal.

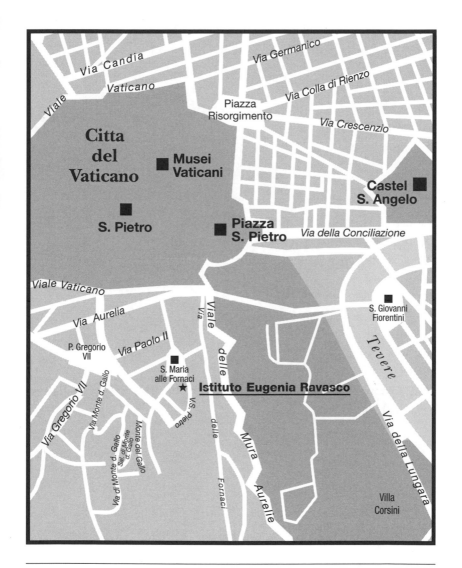

Citta del Vaticano

Via Candia

Viale Vaticano

Via Germanico

Via Colla di Rienzo

Piazza Risorgimento

Via Crescenzio

Musei Vaticani

Castel S. Angelo

S. Pietro

Piazza S. Pietro

Via della Conciliazione

Viale Vaticano

Via Aurelia

Via

Viale

S. Giovanni Fiorentini

P. Gregorio VII

Via Paolo II

delle

Tevere

Via Gregorio VII

Via Monte d. Gallo

Sal. di Monte d. Gallo

Monte del Gallo

S. Maria alle Fornaci

V.S. Pietro

★ Istituto Eugenia Ravasco

delle

Mura

Via della Lungara

Fornaci

Aurelie

Villa Corsini

Istituto Religiose Orsoline
Via Nomentana, 34
Rome 00161 (Roma)
Tel. (06) 440 2953 ▪ Fax (06) 440 04719

The Ursuline sisters have opened their large, Roman home for university students and tourists alike. Everything is clean, simple and updated within the house, which is on a vibrant street just ten minutes from the Via Veneto. Its convenience to public transportation provides easy access to all parts of the city.

Rooms: 24 singles and doubles; half with bath.
Meals: Half or full board available upon request.
Price: 55.000L per person.
Credit cards: Not accepted.
Curfew: 10:30 P.M.
Language(s) spoken: No English.
Facilities: Elevator, chapel.
Season: Open all year.
DIRECTIONS:
Train station: Termini. Take bus no. 36 or 36/ (this is actually a bus number) to Via Nomentana.

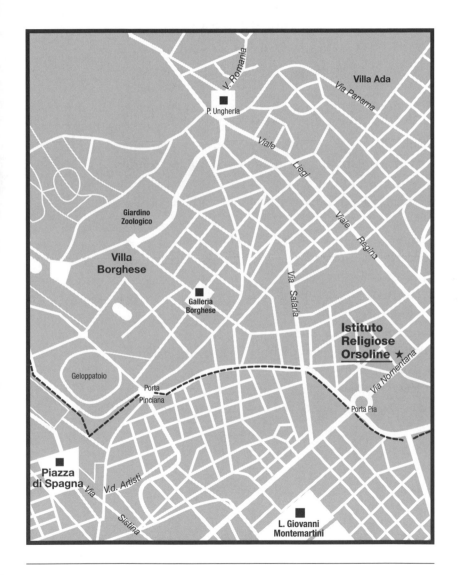

Istituto San Tomasso

Viale Romania, 7

Rome 00196 (Roma)

Tel. (06) 807 0274 ▪ Fax (06) 807 246

Behind imposing wooden doors of an antiquated, austere building is this quiet oasis in the thriving, elegant Parioli district of Rome. The large marble foyer opens onto a peaceful, colorful garden that many of the modernized rooms overlook. The public rooms are fine but have a rather institutional feeling. Restaurant, shops and good transportation are readily accessible.

Rooms: 51 singles and doubles; all with bath.
Meals: Breakfast included.
Price: 80.000L per person.
Credit cards: Not accepted.
Curfew: 10:00 P.M.
Language(s) spoken: French.
Facilities: Parking, elevator, meeting room, chapel.
Season: Open all year.
DIRECTIONS:
Train station: Termini: Take bus no. 4; get off at Viale Romania.

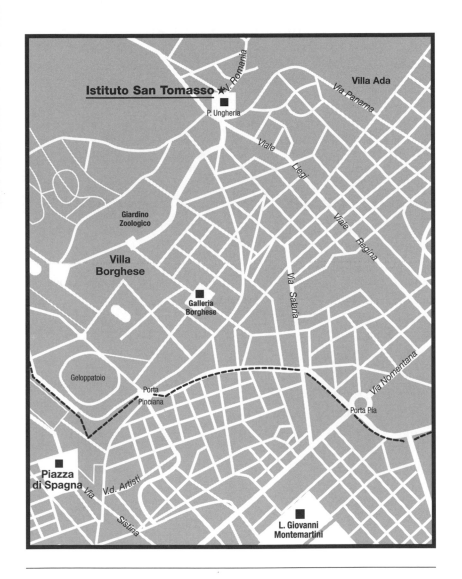

Istituto Santa Giulianna Falconieri
Via Calasanzio, 1
Rome 00186 (Roma)
Tel. (06) 688 03344 ▪ Fax (06) 687 1471

For more than five hundred years, this palazzo and those adjacent to it were owned by a prestigious Roman family. In 1920, the sisters took possession and, in recent years, have opened the house to visitors. There are large, grand public rooms filled with antiques and sprinkled with plants. The upstairs rooms are clean and simple, with modern bathrooms on the floors. Close to the Pantheon, Piazza Navona, Campo dei Fiori, antique shops and restaurants, the location is terrific.

Rooms: Singles, doubles and triples; most with private baths located outside (adjacent to) rooms; telephones in rooms.
Meals: Breakfast included.
Price: 55.000L (single); 90.000L (double); 135.000L (triple).
Credit cards: Not accepted.
Curfew: 11:00 P.M.; 11:30 P.M. Fridays and Saturdays.
Language(s) spoken: English.
Facilities: Elevator, TV room, chapel.
Season: Open all year except August.
DIRECTIONS:
Train station: Termini. Take bus no. 64 to S. Andrea della Valle.

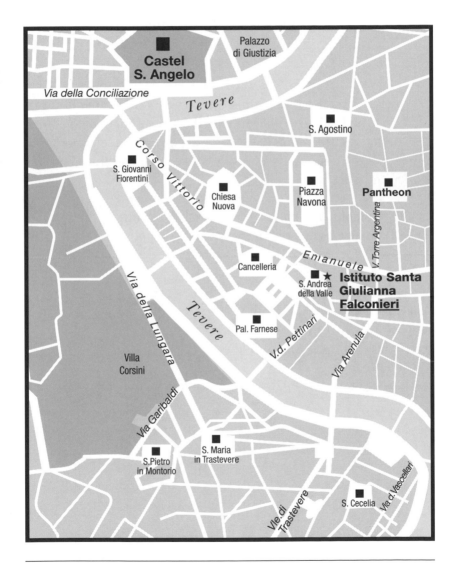

Castel
S. Angelo

Palazzo
di Giustizia

Via della Conciliazione

Tevere

S. Agostino

Corso Vittorio

S. Giovanni
Fiorentini

Chiesa
Nuova

Piazza
Navona

Pantheon

V. Torre Argentina

Emanuele

Cancelleria

S. Andrea
della Valle

★ Istituto Santa
Giulianna
Falconieri

Tevere

Pal. Farnese

V.d. Pettinari

Via Arenula

Via della Lungara

Villa
Corsini

Via Garibaldi

S.Pietro
in Montorio

S. Maria
in Trastevere

Vle. di Trastevere

S. Cecelia

Via d.Vascellari

Mercedarie della Carita
Via Iberia, 8
Rome 00183 (Roma)
Tel. (06) 772 69000 ▪ Fax (06) 772 69092

Operated by delightful nuns, this very modern guesthouse is clean and efficient. There are tiled floors throughout the building, and most of the rooms have large balconies. The neighborhood, however, is marginal, and we would not recommend this house for women traveling alone.

Rooms: 36 singles, doubles and triples; all with bath.
Meals: Breakfast included; full board available upon request.
Price: 50.000L per person.
Credit cards: Not accepted.
Curfew: 11:00 P.M.
Language(s) spoken: No English.
Facilities: Elevator, TV room, meeting room, chapel.
Season: Open all year except August.
DIRECTIONS:
Train station: Termini. Take bus no. 4 to Piazza Tuscolo.

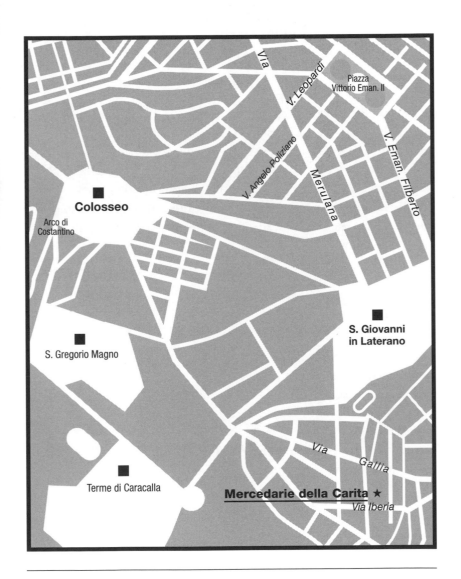

Monastero di S. Maria dei Sette Dolori
Via Garibaldi, 27
Rome 00153 (Roma)
Tel. (06) 589 7327

On the northwest edge of the Trastevere district, set back from the main road and entered through large gates, there is an ancient gray monastery that now welcomes pilgrims and tourists. During the academic year this place is a hub of activity, as several students usually stay here. The accommodations are extremely simple, but the building itself is amazing inside and out. The monastery is a fair walk from the bus stop, so a taxi might be the best transportation when arriving with luggage.

Rooms: 27 singles and doubles; a few with bath.
Meals: Half board only.
Price: 60.000L per person.
Credit cards: Not accepted.
Curfew: 11:00 P.M.
Language(s) spoken: Some English.
Facilities: Parking, elevator, TV room, chapel.
Season: Open all year except August and November.
DIRECTIONS:
Train station: Termini. Take bus no. 75 to Ponte Garibaldi, walk up to Ponte Sisto and turn left.

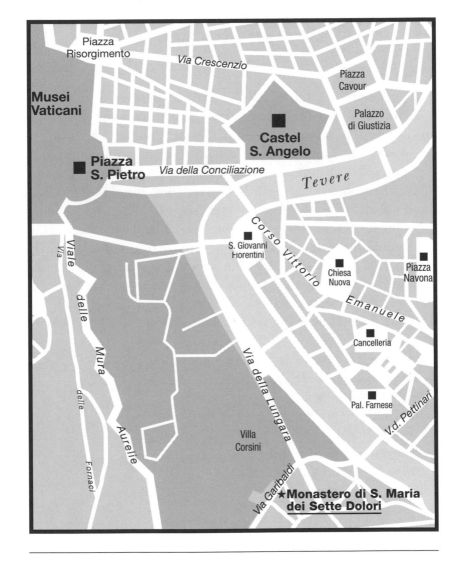

Nostra Signora di Lourdes
Via Sistina, 113
Rome 00187 (Roma)
Tel. (06) 474 5324 ▪ Fax (06) 474 1422

The Sisters of Lourdes run a beautiful guesthouse on the Via Sistina, one of the arterial roads leading from the top of the Spanish Steps down to the Piazza Barberini. Although hardly any of the sisters speak English, there is usually a woman on the front desk during the day who speaks some English. A caveat: They impose a strict curfew on residents—10:30 P.M., and they mean business. But there's plenty of good news, however. You can't fault the location: down the street from the deluxe Hotel Hassler and a few doors from the Inter-Continental. Although the rooms are small and simple, most have private, modern baths. Ask for a room facing the interior courtyard to avoid the din of scooters flying along the Via Sistina at all hours. A rooftop terrace offers spectacular city views, and downstairs you will find peace and quiet in the chapel.

Rooms: Singles, doubles and triples; most with bath.
Meals: Breakfast included.
Price: 50.000L per person.
Credit cards: Not accepted.
Curfew: 10:30 P.M.
Language(s) spoken: French.
Facilities: Elevator, TV room, chapel.
Season: Open all year.

DIRECTIONS:

Train station: Termini. Take metro A to Barberini and walk up the hill to Via Sistina.

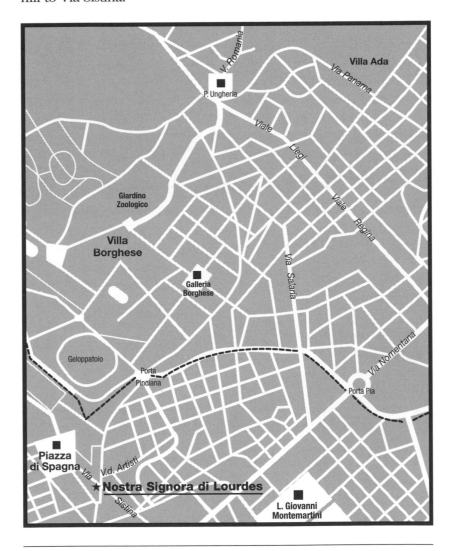

San Giuseppe della Montagna
Viale Vaticano, 88
Rome 00165 (Roma)
Tel. (06) 397 23807 ▪ Fax (06) 397 39095

On the parklike grounds of this complex are both a convent and a seminary. The sisters, who speak Spanish and Italian, are extremely kind, and while they do not speak English, they will gladly find someone who does. The halls and rooms are simple but nicely done. The location is excellent: away from the throngs of people but just a short walk from the genuine splendors of the Vatican Museums.

Rooms: 15 doubles and triples; all with bath.
Meals: Breakfast included.
Price: 50.000L per person.
Credit cards: Not accepted.
Curfew: Flexible.
Language(s) spoken: Some English, Spanish.
Facilities: Chapel.
Season: Open all year.
DIRECTIONS:
Train station: Termini. Take metro A to Ottaviano/S. Pietro, walk toward Vatican and Viale Vaticano is on the right.

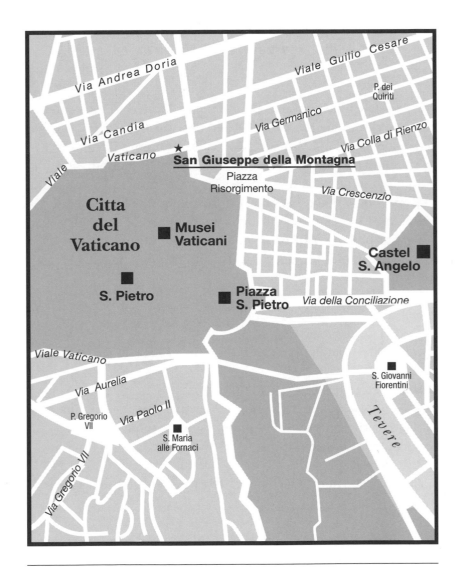

Via Andrea Doria

Viale Guilio Cesare

P. dei
Quiriti

Via Candia

Via Germanico

Viale

Vaticano

Via Colla di Rienzo

★ **San Giuseppe della Montagna**

Piazza
Risorgimento

Via Crescenzio

**Citta
del
Vaticano**

■ **Musei
Vaticani**

**Castel
S. Angelo** ■

■

S. Pietro

■ **Piazza
S. Pietro**

Via della Conciliazione

Viale Vaticano

Via Aurelia

S. Giovanni
Fiorentini ■

P. Gregorio
VII

Via Paolo II

Tevere

S. Maria
alle Fornaci

Via Gregorio VII

San Giuseppe di Cluny
Via Angelo Poliziano, 38
Rome 00184 (Roma)
Tel. (06) 487 2837 ▪ Fax (06) 487 2838

This delightful convent is conveniently located in the center of the city on the Esquiline Hill and near the Colosseum. Situated between Santa Maria Maggiore, where Gian Lorenzo Bernini, one of Italy's most important baroque architects, is buried, and the "Cathedral of Rome and the World," San Giovanni in Laterano, the convent is on a quiet side street off the major tree-lined avenue Via Merulana. Enter and you will find a walled island of tranquility in an otherwise bustling area of town. The sisters offer nicely furnished rooms, many with antiques. Ask for one overlooking the elegant garden.

Rooms: Singles, doubles and triples; some with bath.
Meals: Breakfast included.
Price: 65.000L (single); 126.000L (double); 150.000L (triple).
Credit cards: Not accepted.
Curfew: 10:00 P.M.; 10:30 P.M. in summer.
Language(s) spoken: English, French, German, Portuguese, Spanish.
Facilities: Parking, elevator, TV room, meeting rooms, chapel.
Season: Open all year.
DIRECTIONS:
Train station: Termini. Take bus no. 16 or no. 714 to Brancaccio.

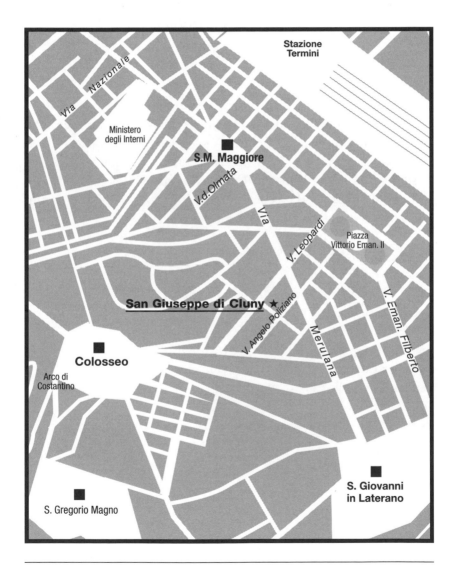

Suore del Buon Salvatore
Via Leopardi, 17
Rome 00185 (Roma)
Tel. (06) 446 7147 ■ Fax (06) 446 1382

The kind sisters who run this guesthouse offer clean, comfortable accommodations. Wrought iron balconies off some of the bedrooms in this delightful convent overlook a small, peaceful garden. The large, yellow stucco house resides on a quiet street in a bustling area in the heart of Rome. Close proximity to shops and restaurants, metro and bus lines, and a short walk to the Colosseum and Forum, make this a convenient place to stay.

Rooms: 39 singles, doubles and triples; all with bath.
Meals: Breakfast included.
Price: 60.000L (single); 110.000L (double); 120.000L (triple).
Credit cards: Not accepted.
Curfew: 10:00 P.M.
Language(s) spoken: English, French, Spanish.
Facilities: Elevator, meeting room, chapel.
Season: Open all year except August.
DIRECTIONS:
Train station: Termini. Take bus no. 16 or no. 714.

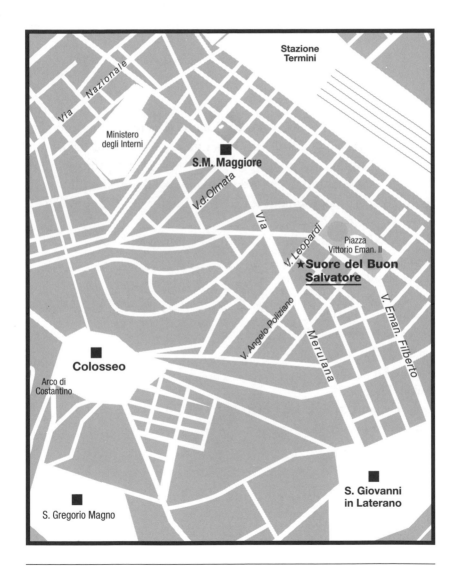

Stazione Termini

Via Nazionale

Ministero degli Interni

S.M. Maggiore

V.d.Olmata

Via

V. Leopardi

Piazza Vittorio Eman. II

★Suore del Buon Salvatore

V. Angelo Poliziano

Merulana

V. Eman. Filberto

Colosseo

Arco di Costantino

S. Giovanni in Laterano

S. Gregorio Magno

**Suore di Corita di S. Maria Dette
del Buon Consiglio
Via Monte del Gallo, 81
Rome 00165 (Roma)
Tel. (06) 393 87388**

Just a few blocks from the Vatican behind a small wrought iron fence is the Suore di Corita di S. Maria Dette del Buon Consiglio. The house is striking, with brown shutters on the pale terra-cotta building. Flowers and enormous palm trees fill the pretty garden. The accommodations are more than adequate, and the phones in each room are a convenient feature not often found in convents.

Rooms: Doubles and triples; all with bath and telephone.
Meals: None.
Price: 40.000L per person.
Credit cards: Not accepted.
Curfew: 10:30 P.M.
Language(s) spoken: No English.
Facilities: Elevator, chapel.
Season: Open all year.
DIRECTIONS:
Train station: Termini. Take bus no. 64 to Vio S. Pio X and then transfer to no. 34.

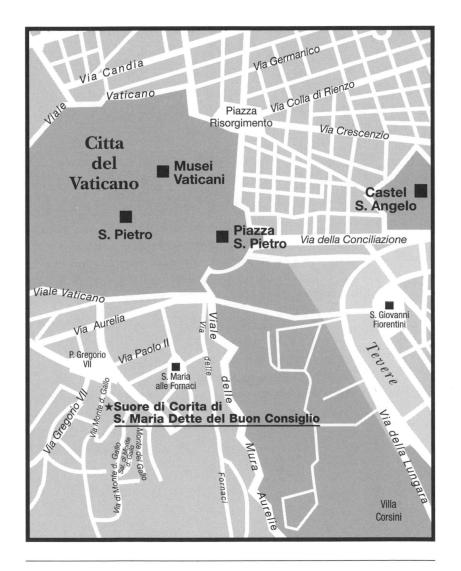

**Suore di Nostra Signora
Del Buon Soccorso
Via degli Artisti, 38
Rome 00187 (Roma)
Tel. (06) 488 5259**

The sisters who run this guesthouse have one of the best loca-
tions in Rome. Close to the metro and bus, all of historic and
artistic Rome is within easy distance. The Via Veneto, Borghese
Gardens, Spanish Steps and wonderful shops and restaurants are
just steps away. The austere gray house is on a short, quiet street in
the center of the city. The rooms are plain but clean and quite
acceptable. Gracious nuns make this house a pleasant place to stay.

Rooms: Singles and doubles; all with bath.
Meals: Breakfast included.
Price: 55.000L per person.
Credit cards: Not accepted.
Curfew: Flexible.
Language(s) spoken: Some English, French.
Facilities: Elevator, chapel.
Season: Open all year.
DIRECTIONS:
Train station: Termini. Take metro A to Barberini.

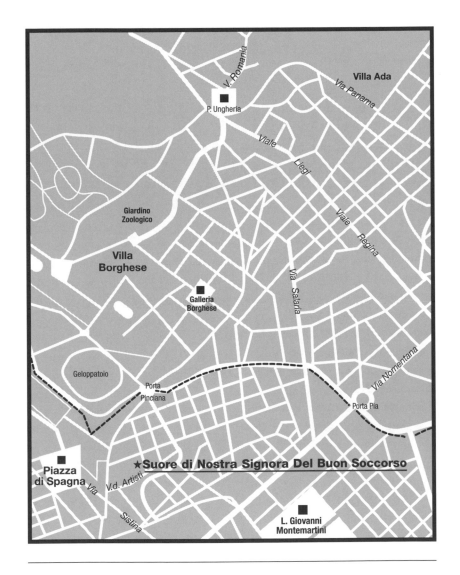

Villa Ada

V. Romania

Via Panama

P. Ungheria

Viale
Liegi

Giardino
Zoologico

Via Regina

Villa
Borghese

Via Salaria

Galleria
Borghese

Via Nomentana

Geloppatoio

Porta
Pinciana

Porta Pia

★Suore di Nostra Signora Del Buon Soccorso

Piazza
di Spagna

Via

V.d. Artisti

Sistina

L. Giovanni
Montemartini

Suore Missionarie Pallottine

Viale delle Mura Aurelie, 7/b

Rome 00165 (Roma)

Tel. (06) 638 6058 ▪ Fax (06) 635 697

U p the hill from Saint Peter's, this modern guesthouse is run by the Pallottine Missionary Sisters. Across from a large park, it is set in a peaceful, quiet area. Sparkling clean, all the rooms are comfortable and many offer large balconies. For visitors' convenience, there is a case near the front desk that sells water, soda and even wine.

Rooms: 29 singles and doubles; a few with bath.
Meals: Breakfast included.
Price: 56.000L (single); 96.000L–140.000L (double).
Credit cards: Not accepted.
Curfew: Flexible.
Language(s) spoken: English, German.
Facilities: Elevator, chapel.
Season: Open all year except July 15–August 31.
DIRECTIONS:
Train station: Termini. Take bus no. 65 to V. Largo di Porta Cavalleggeri.

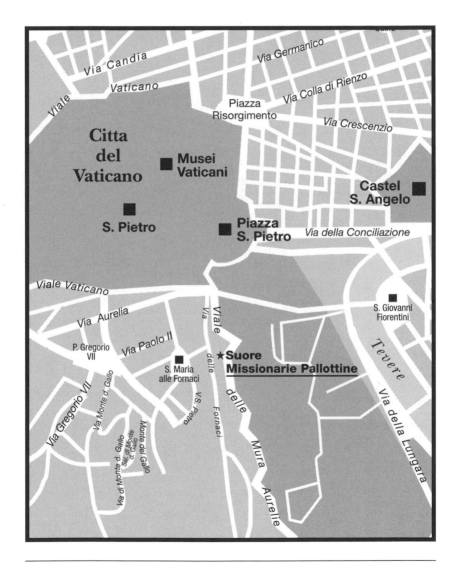

Suore Pie Operaie
Via di Torre Argentina, 76
Rome 00186 (Roma)
Tel. (06) 686 1254

The sisters accept women only in this small, clean, austere pensione. The convent has no amenities whatsoever, but is included because of its location and price. Almost everything in the historical center of Rome is within walking distance, including an excavation of ancient temples. According to legend, it was at the end of this street, Via di Torre Argentina, where Julius Caesar was murdered.

Rooms: Doubles and triples for women only; none with bath.
Meals: None.
Price: 25.000L per person.
Credit cards: Not accepted.
Curfew: 10:30 P.M.
Language(s) spoken: No English.
Facilities: Chapel.
Season: Open all year except August.
DIRECTIONS:
Train station: Termini. Take bus no. 64 to Largo Torre Argentina.

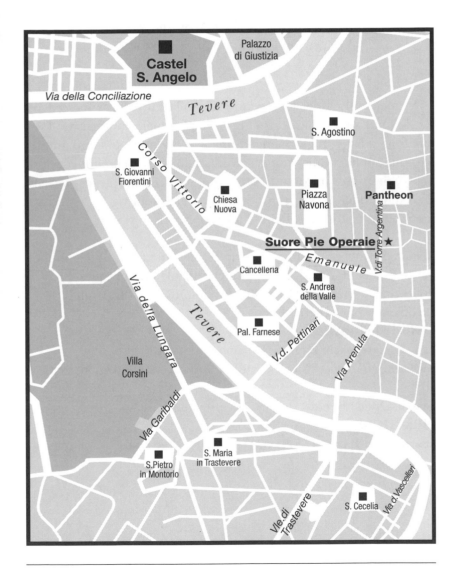

Palazzo
di Giustizia

**Castel
S. Angelo**

Via della Conciliazione

Tevere

S. Agostino

Corso Vittorio

S. Giovanni
Fiorentini

Chiesa
Nuova

Piazza
Navona

Pantheon

V.di Torre Argentina

Suore Pie Operaie ★

Emanuele

Cancelleria

S. Andrea
della Valle

Via della Lungara

Tevere

Pal. Farnese

V.d. Pettinari

Via Arenula

Villa
Corsini

Via Garibaldi

S. Maria
in Trastevere

S.Pietro
in Montorio

Vle.di Trastevere

S. Cecelia

Via d. Vascellari

Villa Lituania
Piazza Aste, 25
Rome 00182 (Roma)
Tel. (06) 701 7464 ■ Fax (06) 701 7468

A medieval castle, turrets and all, Villa Lituania is located on Rome's busy Piazza Aste. Entering from an unobtrusive door, one finds a large, high-ceilinged hall that opens on to large, unpretentious public rooms. The accommodations are plain but comfortable. Guests are welcome to enjoy the terrace and pretty gardens. Proximity to all public transportation makes touring Rome convenient. Everyone is most helpful and courteous to visitors.

Rooms: 57 singles, doubles and triples; all with bath and telephone.
Meals: Breakfast included; full board available upon request.
Price: 75.000L (single); 130.000L (double); 195.000L (triple).
Credit cards: Not accepted.
Curfew: 11:00 P.M.
Language(s) spoken: English, German and Portuguese.
Facilities: Parking (extra), elevator, TV room, meeting room, bar, chapel.
Season: Open all year.
DIRECTIONS:
Train station: Termini. Take metro A to Re di Roma.

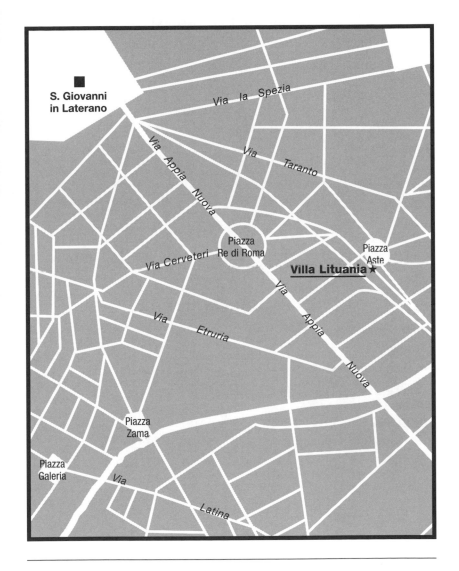

S. Giovanni in Laterano

Via la Spezia

Via Appia Nuova

Via Taranto

Via Cerveteri

Piazza Re di Roma

Piazza Aste

Villa Lituania ★

Via Appia Nuova

Via Etruria

Piazza Zama

Piazza Galeria

Via

Via Latina

Villa Noel

Via Andrea Doria, 42

Rome 00192 (Roma)

Tel. (06) 397 37020 ▪ Fax (06) 397 37020

The attractive gray stone villa of the Suore Oblate dell'Assunzione is set behind wrought iron gates that open on to a palm-filled garden neatly divided by a cobblestone path leading to the entrance. Inside, the warmth and graciousness of the sisters allow one to overlook the refurbishing needs of this clean old convent. Located in a busy area filled with shops and restaurants, visitors can easily walk the few blocks to the metro and Saint Peter's Basilica.

Rooms: Singles, doubles and two private apartments; none with bath except apartments.
Meals: None.
Price: 45.000L (single); 80.000L (double).
Credit cards: Not accepted.
Curfew: 10:30 P.M.
Language(s) spoken: French.
Facilities: Elevator, TV room, chapel.
Season: Open all year.
DIRECTIONS:
Train station: Termini. Take metro A to Ottaviano/S. Pietro.

The cloister garden of **San Giuseppe di Cluny**, Rome

ERIN WALSH

Villa Charles Garnier in Bordighera on the Ligurian coast

MIKE WALSH

Garden entrance at
Villa Maria Elisabetta,
Lake Garda

Casa del Terziario,
once a sixteenth-century palazzo, Assisi

Balcony view from a bedroom in **Albergo Domus Mariae** in Siracusa, Sicily

The dining room at **Il Carmine** in San Felice del Benaco, Lake Garda

View of the Dolomites from
the terrace of **Dolomiti Pio X**
in Borca di Cadore

ANNE WALSH

Doorway to **Istituto San Giuseppe**,
near the Ponte della Guerra in Venice

ANNE WALSH

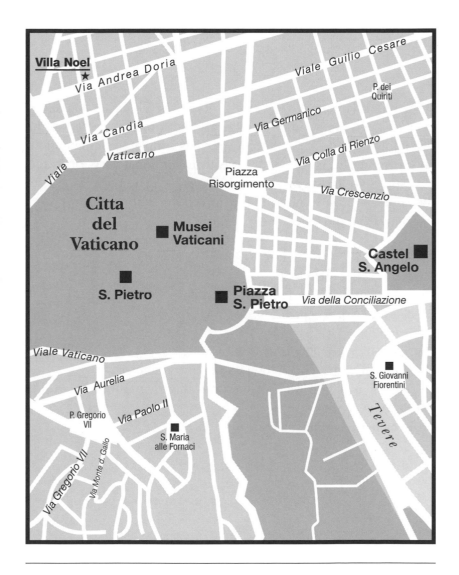

Villa Rosa
Via Terme Deciane, 5
Rome 00153 (Roma)
Tel. (06) 574 3793 ▪ Fax (06) 574 5275

Dominican nuns run this lovely villa for their international sisters and as a guesthouse for pilgrims and tourists. Located in the beautiful Aventine area, the convent has simple accommodations and a wonderful garden terrace with exceptional views of Rome. The sisters are most gracious and hospitable. The bus that goes to the center of Rome and to many attractions in the city stops just a few steps from the house.

Rooms: Singles, doubles and triples; all with bath.
Meals: Breakfast included.
Price: 75.000L (single); 110.000L (double); 150.000L (triple).
Credit cards: Not accepted.
Curfew: None.
Language(s) spoken: English.
Facilities: Parking, elevator, TV room, library, chapel.
Season: Open all year except Christmas and the month of August.
DIRECTIONS:
Train station: Termini. Take bus no. 175.

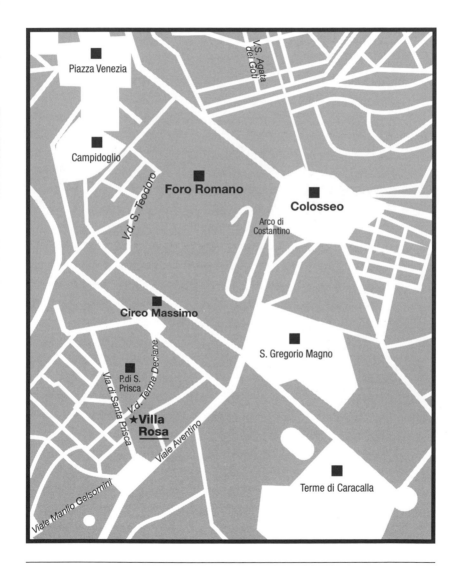

NOTES

LIGURIA

Stretching along the Mediterranean from Ventimiglia, near the French border, to La Spezia on the east, Liguria is a bevy of small towns and villages anchored by its historic capital, Genoa. The Romans built the original Via Aurelia, the road that runs along most of the coast, but the capital was already a thriving seaport before their arrival three centuries before Christ. For the next several hundred years, the prominence of this port brought prestige, fame and wealth to this region. In time the region declined as Genoa became a less important power. When the Kingdom of Italy came into being, however, Liguria began a slow rebirth.

Liguria is a prosperous area supported by commercial enterprises, the bustling port of Genoa, a thriving flower industry and tourism. Blessed by an incomparable climate, the sun-drenched coastal towns, backed by mountain slopes, surrounded by fragrant flowers and trees and located on the shimmering Mediterranean, are an incredible draw for old and young, rich and poor.

Bordighera, at the far western end of Liguria, was the playground of British royalty around the turn of the last century. Cute shops, good restaurants, a boat basin and a grand beach promenade make a visit to this sophisticated little town a real treat. The city is also designated as the provider of Holy Week palms to the Vatican.

Just a few kilometers east is San Remo, once an elegant resort, presently a large commercial city with massive, old hotels, a municipal casino and plenty of night life. Most famous as the flower capital of Italy, its flower market should not be missed.

Not far from San Remo, a much quieter spot is available. Diano Marina is a small resort with good beaches and small shops and cafes. Farther along the coast, Alassio is the real gem on the Riviera di Ponente. A bustling resort, it is an obvious favorite of Europeans. Hundreds of umbrellas contribute to a kaleidoscope of colors from one end of the city's great beach to the other. A broad promenade adds to the festive feeling, as do the delightful cafes and little specialty shops.

Loano is a good-sized town situated by the bright blue Mediterranean and backed by mountains. If you tire of the beach life, plenty of shops and quaint restaurants are available.

Varigotti is a tiny seaside town with a few good shops and restaurants; it is a clean, convenient stop if the other towns are crowded.

Noli and Spotorno are almost side by side in this area known as La Riviera delle Palme. Spotorno, the larger enclave favored by Europeans, is a small, quaint town dedicated to sun and leisure. Noli is more interesting from a historical viewpoint, as it was once a wealthy medieval city-state. Good weather and excellent beaches make it a real drawing card.

Set against a backdrop of hills, with the sea lapping at its shores, Pietra Ligure offers a perfect vacation spot for those who enjoy tiled-roof villas, large palm trees, lovely flowers, gaily colored beach umbrellas and unparalleled views of the sea.

Beyond the frenetic pace of Genoa, the quiet towns of the eastern end of the Ligurian coast appear. Santa Margherita Ligure, one of the first, is a wonderful, unspoiled town on the sea. Small boats bounce in the harbor fronted by a grand palm-filled public park. Beaches, cafes, churches and shops are just steps away, and Portofino, the little fishing village once owned by Benedictine friars and now a sophisticated, world-renowned resort, is reachable by car or ferry.

Down the highway, Rapallo, a big resort past its prime, is still a vibrant vacation town on the water. For years, the harbor views, palm-lined streets and wonderful climate have drawn artists, writers and tourists. Part of the town retains its medieval buildings, where art and antique lace are available in some of the tiny shops. Another attraction is the funicular ride to the Sanctuary of the Madonna of Montallegro. Floating over rooftops and forested hills in a petite cable car, one arrives at the mountaintop home of the magnificent sixteenth-century church overlooking the sparkling Gulf of Genoa.

South of Rapallo, the small town of Levanto hugs the hillside at the water's edge. Dating back to A.D. 730, it was once a home to Franciscan and Augustinian monasteries. Today, it is a quiet coastal resort with thirteenth-century buildings and attractive beaches.

Cinque Terre is a group of five fishing villages at the southern end of Liguria. Situated on a hillside and extremely difficult to reach, these little villages are unspoiled delights of fragrant olive and citrus groves on terraced hills, medieval churches, wonderful views and a simple lifestyle. Monterosso is the largest of the five towns; sitting at the bottom of a lush hill, it offers a lively town center with restaurants, cafes and shops and several small beaches. This is a perfect place from which to explore the four other villages by train or on foot.

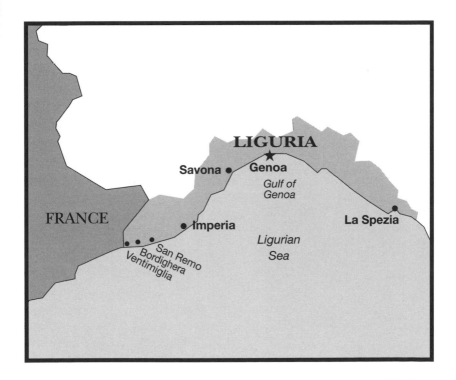

Alassio

Casa San Domenico
Via Rome, 87
Alassio 17021 (Savona)
Tel. (0182) 642 01/645 198 ▪ Fax (0182) 642 01

Casa San Domenico is an incredibly beautiful three-story Italian villa set in a lush garden of flowers and palm trees directly across from the beach. The public rooms are filled with antiques, and the airy dining room faces the sea. The accommodations are simple, but a few have balconies overlooking the Mediterranean.

Rooms: 15 singles, doubles and triples; most with bath.
Meals: Full board only.
Price: 55.000L–95.000L per person, depending on season and view.
Credit cards: Not accepted.
Curfew: 11:00 P.M.
Language(s) spoken: English.
Facilities: Parking, elevator, TV room, chapel.
Season: Open January to mid-October.
DIRECTIONS:
Train: Alassio, then take a taxi.
Car: A10; exit Alassio. V. Roma is the beach road at the western end of town.

Bordighera

Beau Rivage
Via Aurelia, 47
Bordighera 18012 (Imperia)
Tel. (0184) 261 577 ■ Fax (0184) 254 907

Beau Rivage is a modest four-story house in a semicommercial area at the western end of Bordighera. Adjacent to a good beach, many of the rooms have wonderful views of the house's beautiful garden and the sparkling Mediterranean beyond. Noise, however, can be a problem due to its proximity to the railroad tracks.

Rooms: 25 singles, doubles and triples; most with bath.
Meals: Breakfast included; half and full board available upon request.
Price: 55.000L (single); 65.000L (double).
Credit cards: Not accepted.
Curfew: 10:30 P.M.
Language(s) spoken: No English.
Facilities: Parking, elevator, TV room, library, chapel.
Season: Open all year except October and November.
DIRECTIONS:
Train station: Bordighera. Take a taxi to the convent.
Car: A10, exit Bordighera and proceed south to Via Aurelia.

Villa Charles Garnier

Via C. Garnier, 11

Bordighera 18012 (Imperia)

Tel. (0184) 261 833

In the latter part of the nineteenth century, the original owner of this elegant villa was Charles Garnier, architect of the neo-baroque Paris Opera House. Upon his death he left the house to the Sisters of Saint Joseph, who today run a gracious, hospitable house for visitors. The main rooms are furnished with antiques, many of which Garnier purchased for the house. Most of the accommodations have balconies with views of the glistening blue sea, and, on the outside, broad tiled terraces edged with flowers overlook the busy marina below. The villa is a charming oasis on the Italian Riviera and the director, Sister Giovanna Maria, could not be more gracious or hospitable.

Rooms: 16 singles and doubles; all with bath.
Meals: Full board only.
Price: 70.000L (single); 65.000L (double) per person.
Credit cards: Not accepted.
Curfew: Flexible.
Language(s) spoken: No English.
Facilities: Limited parking, meeting rooms, chapel.
Season: Christmas–mid-October.
DIRECTIONS:
Train station: Bordighera. Take a taxi to the convent.
Car: At the eastern end of Bordighera from Via Arziglia, take Via Garnier up the hill to no. 11.

Villa Serena
Via V. Veneto, 60
Bordighera 16035 (Imperia)
Tel. (0184) 261 634

A gigantic arc of pink bougainvillaea stands at the pretty gated entrance of Villa Serena. A lovely garden surrounds the white stone house, and inside the rooms are plain but quite comfortable. The location is excellent—just a short walk to the beach and the quaint shops and restaurants of this picturesque town.

Rooms: 28 singles and doubles; all with bath.
Meals: Breakfast included; full board available upon request.
Price: 67.000L–75.000L per person, depending upon the season.
Credit cards: Not accepted.
Curfew: 11:00 P.M.
Language(s) spoken: Some English.
Facilities: Elevator, TV room.
Season: Open all year.
DIRECTIONS:
Train station: Bordighera. Take a taxi or walk.
Car: A10, exit Bordighera to Via Vittorio Emanuel and turn north on Via Vittoria Veneto.

Diano Marina

Soggiorno Don Orione
Via Divina Provvidenza, 1
Diano Marina 18013 (Imperia)
Tel. (0183) 498 108 ▪ Fax (0183) 498 006

High on a hill above the Ligurian coast, this holiday house offers peace and tranquility. Pale pink stucco buildings are set in a small park filled with grass, flowers and trees. The public rooms and accommodations are plain, but most of the latter have balconies with wonderful views of the sparkling Mediterranean. The casa is some distance from the lively little town of Diano Marina, where you will find typical beach scenes of bathers, sun worshipers and colorful beach umbrellas.

Rooms: 50 singles, doubles and triples; all with bath and telephone.
Meals: Breakfast included.
Price: 52.000L–60.000L.
Credit cards: Not accepted.
Curfew: Flexible.
Language(s) spoken: No English.
Facilities: Parking, elevator, TV room, four handicapped rooms available, bar, meeting rooms, chapel.
Season: Open all year.
DIRECTIONS:
Train station: Diano Marina. Take a taxi.
Car: From the western end of town head north on Via D. Provvidenza from Via Aurelia. It is a long, winding road to no. 1.

Levanto

Villa Rossana
Via Valle Santa, 7
Levanto 19015 (La Spezia)
Tel. (0187) 808 281

On the Ligurian coast, the gracious nuns of "Buon Pastore" run a very pleasant two-star hotel. Their pale yellow villa set against a lush green hillside contains a garden of pine and palm trees located directly across from the beach. The accommodations are comfortable, many of the rooms have sea views and a few have balconies. It is an easy walk to town, and the nearby villages of Cinque Terre are easily accessible by train or foot.

Rooms: 27 singles and doubles; all with bath.
Meals: Breakfast included; half and full board available upon request.
Price: 78.000L–86.000L per room, depending on the season.
Credit cards: Not accepted.
Curfew: 11:00 P.M.
Language(s) spoken: No English.
Facilities: Parking, elevator, TV room, chapel.
Season: Open all year.
DIRECTIONS:
Train station: Levanto. Take a taxi.
Car: From A12, exit Brugnato or Carrodano and follow signs to Levanto. Proceed to beachfront road and head west. Villa Rossana is on the right at the far end of the road.

Loano

Istituto San Giuseppe
Via Carducci, 20
Loano 17025 (Savona)
Tel. (019) 670 793

At the foot of the rolling Ligurian hills an orchard of fragrant lemon trees surrounds this red-roofed three-story Italian villa. Run by delightful nuns, the interior of the house is spotless, comfortable and quite pretty. Within walking distance of the beach, the villa is also close to the little town of Loano, which is filled with specialty shops and gaily decorated restaurants.

Rooms: 60 singles and doubles (for families and single women only); all with bath.
Meals: Breakfast included; full board available upon request.
Price: 52.000L–54.000L per person.
Credit cards: Not accepted.
Curfew: Flexible.
Language(s) spoken: No English.
Facilities: Parking.
Season: Open all year except November and December.
DIRECTIONS:
Train station: Loano. Take taxi or walk to the convent.
Car: A10 to Via Aurelia. Head west to Via Carducci and turn right.

Montallegro

Casa del Pellegrino
Viale Santurio, 15
Montallegro 16035 (Genoa)
Tel. (0185) 239 003 ▪ Fax (0185) 239 003

On a hill above Rappallo is a large, lovely sixteenth-century church with a magnificent Byzantine Madonna. The city celebrates the feast of "The Madonna of Montallegro" with great festivities during the first three days of July. Behind the church, a pretty hillside path leads to a pink stucco casa for pilgrims and visitors. Set amongst the trees, with the feeling of an old country house, it offers plain rooms and a great terrace for dining, relaxing and spectacular views. For a grand experience, take the small funicular to the top— it is a quick ride and you will be rewarded with incredible vistas.

Rooms: 39 singles, doubles and triples; some with bath.
Meals: Breakfast included; half and full board available upon request.
Price: 45.000L per person.
Credit cards: Not accepted.
Curfew: No.
Language(s) spoken: No English.
Facilities: Parking, TV room, restaurant, bar, laundry, chapel.
Season: Easter through summer.
DIRECTIONS:
Train station: Rapallo. Take a taxi to the funicular.
Car: A12, exit Sanctuario di Montallegro.

Monterosso al Mare

Soggiorno Padre G. Semeria
Viale P. G. Semeria, 35
Monterosso al Mare 19016 (La Spezia)
Tel. (0187) 818 192

Set in a park on the hillside just above Monterosso is a large, beige stucco complex offering hospitality to groups and individuals. The public rooms and accommodations are clean, plain and utilitarian. Several of the rooms have sea views, and the fourteen small bungalows would be good for families and small groups. This is a fine location for anyone wishing to explore Cinque Terre.

Rooms: Singles and doubles and 14 apartments; most with bath.
Meals: Breakfast included; half and full board available upon request.
Price: 22.000L–60.000L per person, depending upon meals.
Credit cards: Not accepted.
Curfew: 10:30 P.M.
Language(s) spoken: Some English.
Facilities: Parking, elevator, TV room, chapel.
Season: Open all year.
DIRECTIONS:
Train station: Monterosso. Take a taxi.
Car: A12, exit Carodgno. Follow signs to Monterosso. The house is on the right side just before you reach the town center.

Villa Adriana
Via IV Novembre, 5
Monterosso al Mare 19016 (La Spezia)
Tel. (0187) 818 109 ■ Fax (0187) 818 128

Sitting unobtrusively behind wrought iron gates in a gorgeous tropical garden is Villa Adriana. This late-nineteenth-century house has fine accommodations, several with views of the spectacular Gulf of Genoa, pretty public rooms and access to a private beach. The lively town is about two blocks away, and the four other charming fishing villages that comprise Cinque Terre are quite accessible.

Rooms: 54 singles and doubles; all with bath and telephone.
Meals: Breakfast included; half and full board available upon request.
Price: 65.000L–105.000L per person, depending upon the season.
Credit cards: Not accepted.
Curfew: 11:00 P.M.
Language(s) spoken: English.
Facilities: Parking, elevator, TV room, bar, chapel.
Season: Open March 1–October 30.
DIRECTIONS:
Train station: Monterosso. Take a taxi.
Car: A12, exit Carrocano and follow signs to Monterosso. Proceed to beach road and turn right to Via IV Novembre.

Noli

Casa al Mare dell'Incoronata
Regione Torbora, 1
Noli 17026 (Savona)
Tel. (019) 748 810 ▪ Fax (019) 748 810

From a distance, this casa appears to be a red medieval castle; up close it turns into a large, interesting building with many nooks and crannies. Set on a hill at the western end of Noli (a town mentioned in Dante's *Divine Comedy*), it provides grand views of the spectacular coast. About half the rooms have balconies facing the sea, the public rooms are very nice, the gardens are large and well-maintained and the sisters will make beach reservations for guests.

Rooms: 33 singles, doubles and triples; 30 with bath.
Meals: Breakfast included; full board available upon request.
Price: 43.000L–65.000L.
Credit cards: Not accepted.
Curfew: Flexible.
Language(s) spoken: No English.
Facilities: Parking, elevator, TV room, meeting rooms, restaurant, bar, chapel.
Season: Open summer only.
DIRECTIONS:
Train station: Spotorno. Take a local bus to Noli, and then take a taxi.
Car: From Noli center, go west on Via Aurelia and look for the castlelike building on the hill. Turn right at the Casa's sign.

Istituto Madre Pie
Via Cesari, 2
Noli 17026 (Savona)
Tel. (019) 748 475/748 906

While they speak no English, the sisters at Istituto Madre Pie could not be more delightful or hospitable. Situated across from a fine beach, the pink stucco villa sits behind wrought iron gates in a lovely garden of pink flowers and palm trees. Several rooms face the water, the public rooms are quite attractive and a brick terrace is available for all guests. A few interesting medieval churches and buildings are just footsteps away.

Rooms: 21 singles and doubles; all with bath.
Meals: Breakfast included; half and full board available.
Price: 60.000L (single); 75.000L (double).
Credit cards: Not accepted.
Curfew: Flexible.
Language(s) spoken: No English.
Facilities: Parking, elevator, TV room, meeting room, restaurant, bar, chapel.
Season: Open all year.
DIRECTIONS:
Train station: Spotorno. Take a local bus to Noli and then take a taxi.

Bed and Blessings: Italy

Pietra Ligure

Albergo Regina Mundi
Viale Europa, 57
Pietra Ligure 17027 (Savona)
Tel. (019) 615 859 ▪ Fax (019) 616 433

G racious sisters greet visitors in the marble reception area of this two-star hotel. Just a block from the beach, many of the rooms have balconies with wonderful views of the glistening blue water. The common rooms are bright and airy, and there is a profusion of palm trees and colorful flowers in the large garden. The only drawback at this delightful holiday house is its close proximity to the train tracks.

Rooms: 43 singles and doubles; all with bath and telephone.
Meals: Breakfast included; half and full board available upon request.
Price: 35.000L– 50.000L (single); 45.000L– 60.000L (double) depending on view.
Credit cards: Not accepted.
Curfew: Flexible.
Language(s) spoken: No English.
Facilities: Parking, elevator, TV room, chapel.
Season: Open from December–September.
DIRECTIONS:
Train station: Finale Ligure. Take a local bus to Pietra Ligure and then take a taxi.
Car: A10, exit Pietra Ligure. Drop down to Via Aurelia, continue to Via Ghirardi, go north one block and turn right on Viale Europa.

Rapallo

Istituto Orsolie di Maria Immacolata
Via Aurelia Levante, 54
Rapallo 16035 (Genoa)
Tel. (0185) 232 014 ▪ Fax (0185) 270 919

The plain stucco facade of this house on a busy road belies the lovely interior and beautiful tropical garden beyond. The dining room and small salon are nicely appointed and overlook the gardens. Several of the simple guest rooms have balconies with views of the glistening Mediterranean. During the academic year the sisters run a school, but visitors are welcome during the summer months. The convent is within walking distance of the busy, festive resort town.

Rooms: Singles and doubles; most with bath.
Meals: Full board only.
Price: 100.000L per person.
Credit cards: Not accepted.
Curfew: 10:30 P.M.
Language(s) spoken: Some English.
Facilities: Elevator, TV room, meeting rooms, chapel.
Season: Open summer only.
DIRECTIONS:
Train station: Rapallo. Take a taxi or local bus to convent.
Car: A12, exit Rappallo and proceed to "Centro." From Piazza Pastene, take V. Montebello, bear right to V. Avenaggi, turn right at Via Aurelia Levante.

Santa Margherita Ligure

Oasi Regina Pacis

Via Pellerano, 6

Santa Margherita Ligure 16038 (Genoa)

Tel. (0185) 286 842

The flowered terraces and many rooms of this guesthouse have beautiful panoramas of the breathtaking Gulf of Santa Margherita. At night, the twinkling lights of Portofino and Rapallo can be seen in the distance. Difficult to reach, the warm welcome of the sisters and the pleasant surroundings make this convent worth the effort.

Rooms: 13 singles and doubles; most with bath.
Meals: Only full board available.
Price: 60.000L per person.
Credit cards: Not accepted.
Curfew: No.
Language(s) spoken: No English.
Facilities: TV room, chapel.
Season: Open all year.
DIRECTIONS:
Train station: S. Margherita Ligure. Take a taxi.
Car: A12, exit Santa Margherita Ligure. Take Via Nicolo Cuneo (in the direction of Recco-Camogli) up to no. 58 (Villa delle Palme). Park car and walk on Via Pellarano (pedestrian street) for approximately 50 yards to no. 6.

Spotorno

Hotel Mazza
Via Acqua Novella, 1
Spotorno 17028 (Savona)
Tel. (019) 745 334 ▪ Fax (019) 746 344

At the far end of Spotorno, the three-star Mazza Hotel sits on a hill with a commanding view of the sea. The flagstone terrace is surrounded by trees, shrubs and flowers. The accommodations are clean and plain, and many have wonderful views of the coastline; sadly, the public rooms have a very institutional appearance. It is a short walk to a good beach.

Rooms: 39 singles and doubles; all with bath and TV.
Meals: Full board only.
Price: 95.000L (single); 85.000L (double) per person; sea-view rooms additional.
Credit cards: Most major.
Curfew: No.
Language(s) spoken: No English.
Facilities: Parking, elevator, televisions in rooms, meeting rooms, restaurant, bar, air conditioning.
Season: Open Easter to mid-October.
DIRECTIONS:
Train station: Spotorno. Take a taxi.
Car: From V. Aurelia, go under railway bridge at eastern end of town, proceed to fork in the road; turn right, bear left at first road and go up the hill to the hotel.

La Conchiglia
Via S. Caterina, 3
Spotorno 17028 (Savona)
Tel. (019) 745 850

La Conchiglia is situated in an old, pretty neighborhood within walking distance of lively Spotorno. The sisters are kind and hospitable, taking special delight in welcoming young families. Tropical gardens surround the house and a small playground is available for children. The interior rooms are attractive and comfortable.

Rooms: 40 singles, doubles and triples (for families and single women only); all with bath and telephone.
Meals: Full board only.
Price: 60.000L per person.
Credit cards: Not accepted.
Curfew: 11:00 P.M.
Language(s) spoken: No English.
Facilities: Parking, elevator, TV room, bar, laundry, chapel.
Season: Open all year.
DIRECTIONS:
Train station: Spotorno. Take a taxi.
Car: A10, exit Spotorno to Via Giuseppe Verdi and then on to Santa Caterina. Take a left to no. 3.

Varigotti

Istituto San Francesco

Strada degli Arenzi, 3

Varigotti 17029 (Savona)

Tel. (019) 698 025

Up a long, winding road on a hill above the Ligurian Coast, Istituto San Francesco is a pretty beige stucco villa. The sisters provide plain, clean accommodations, small public rooms decorated with antiques and fantastic views of shimmering azure sea. The spacious gardens are planted with flowers, grapevines and olive trees. The sisters have access to a private beach in the quaint town of Varigotti, but it is some distance from the convent.

Rooms: 34 singles and doubles; all with bath.
Meals: Breakfast included; full board available upon request.
Price: 48.000L (single); 68.000L (double).
Credit cards: Not accepted.
Curfew: Flexible.
Language(s) spoken: No English.
Facilities: Parking, elevator, TV room, chapel.
Season: Open summer only.
DIRECTIONS:
Car: At the western end of Varigotti, take Via degli Ulivi (one block north of Via Aurelia) to Via degli Arenzi; head north to the convent. (Approximately four kilometers.)

LOMBARDY

Bordering Switzerland on the north, Lombardy is a land of peaks, plains and lakes. The beautiful region was first explored more than three thousand years ago by the Etruscans; from that time forward it was invaded by a succession of conquerors until the twelfth century, when the Lombard League came into power. For the next few hundred years the fighting was internal until 1525, when the Spanish took control for the next two hundred years after the Battle of Pavia. Next came the Austrians, Napoleon, the Austrians again and finally, in 1861, the region became part of the Kingdom of Italy.

The present-day Lombardy is a booming, prosperous, heavily populated region. The capital, Milan, a dynamic urban metropolis, offers a glorious gothic duomo, the famous opera house La Scala and Da Vinci's *Last Supper* among its many points of interest. The area's vibrant economy is supported by fashion design, textiles, agriculture, financial institutions and other kinds of industry, including tourism.

Tourists come to all parts of Lombardy, but the region's magnificent lakes draw the biggest groups. Mentioned by writers from Virgil to Hemingway, each of the lakes offers something special. The most famous is probably Lake Como, but the Italians go in great numbers to the largest one, Lake Garda, a popular resort area since Roman times. There are convents in three towns on the western shores of Garda.

San Felice del Benaco is a small village with a few shops and good beaches. It is a fine place to stop for a more peaceful time than you will find in the bigger lake towns.

Gardone Riviera is a large, lush resort that was once the most elegant and fashionable on the lake. The home of Gabriele d'Annuzio, the famous modern Italian poet, it is still beautiful although a little faded. Good shops, lively cafes and pretty villas line the shores.

Maderno is a great location, as the ferry terminal is located right in the town. The steamers ply the lake to many of the surrounding villages. This is a calm, quiet location with small shops and restaurants that serve delicious food.

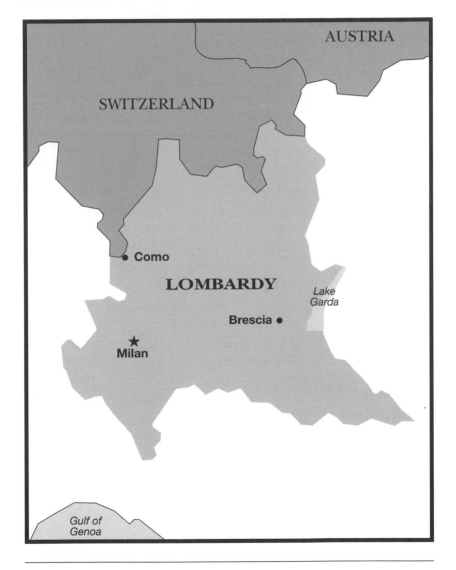

Gardone Riviera

Villa Maria Elisabetta
Viale Zanardelli, 156
Gardone Riviera 25083 (Brescia)
Tel. (0365) 202 06 ■ Fax (0365) 202 06

L ined with tropical trees and shrubs, a long driveway extends to the portals of this beautiful Italian villa. Large, pretty common rooms are on the first floor. Upstairs, the bedrooms are simple, and many have wonderful views of Lake Garda. Spacious grounds and a magnificent gazebo complement the house. Several paths lead to the water's edge, where there is a dazzling terrace with a balustrade adorned with red geraniums. A small ladder is attached for swimming in the lake and a spectacular sundeck is close by. The warm hospitality of the Sisters of Saint Elizabeth is evident upon arrival.

Rooms: Singles, doubles and triples; all with bath.
Meals: Half or full board only.
Price: 68.000L (half board); 74.000L (full board) per person.
Credit cards: Not accepted.
Curfew: Flexible.
Language(s) spoken: Some English, German.
Facilities: Parking, TV room, bar, chapel.
Season: December 1–October 15.
DIRECTIONS:
Train station: Desenzano. Take a local bus to Gardone Riviera.
Car: From A4, exit Desenzano and proceed north on SS 572 to Gardone.

Maderno

Pensione Villa Angela

Via Dante, 13

Maderno 25080 (Brescia)

Tel. (0365) 641 730

Located just a short walk from the lakefront with its lovely park and promenade is a villa run by the Sisters of Sant'Angela Merci. A plain house in a fine residential neighborhood, the pensione has modern accommodations, many with balconies overlooking floral gardens. The charming little town of Maderno, with its delightful shops and restaurants, is three blocks away, making for a pleasant adventure. At the edge of town is a ferry terminal that facilitates day trips to nearby towns and villages.

Rooms: Singles and doubles; all with bath.
Meals: Breakfast included.
Price: 45.000L (single); 55.000L (double).
Credit cards: Not accepted.
Curfew: Flexible.
Language(s) spoken: No English.
Facilities: Parking, TV room, chapel.
Season: Open May 15–September 30.
DIRECTIONS:
Train station: Desenzano. Take local bus to Maderno.
Car: A4, exit Desenzano. Go north on SS 572 to Maderno (approximately 30 kilometers).

San Felice del Benaco

Il Carmine
Via Fontanamonte, 1
San Felice del Benaco 25010 (Brescia)
Tel. (0365) 623 65 ▪ Fax (0365) 623 64

Adjacent to a fifteenth-century Carmelite sanctuary, this large stucco house is entered through a gated doorway guarded by small stone lions. Perched on a slope a short distance from Lake Garda, Il Carmine has several large public rooms, including a vast dining room with a great stone fireplace. The accommodations have been modernized, and many have lake views. In the center of the house is a peaceful cloister and, in the back, a terraced garden surrounded by olive trees. The sisters represent five continents and provide a warm welcome to all.

Rooms: 59 singles, doubles and triples; all with bath.
Meals: Breakfast included; half or full board available upon request.
Price: 50.000L per person; 65.000L (half board); 75.000L (full board) per person.
Credit cards: Not accepted.
Curfew: 11:00 P.M.
Language(s) spoken: Some English.
Facilities: Parking, elevator, TV room, meeting rooms, restaurant, bar, chapel.
Season: Open all year.
DIRECTIONS:
Car: A5, exit Desenzano, go north 16 kilometers and watch for signs to San Felice and/or Santuario delle Madonna del Carmine.

NOTES

MARCHES

Marches is a small region in the middle of Italy. The capital is Ancona, a seaside town founded in the fourth century B.C. by Siracusans. The area was taken over by the Romans in the following century and subsequently invaded by the Byzantines, Lombards and other conquerors until 1532, when the Catholic Church annexed it as a papal state. It remained that way until 1860, when it became part of the Kingdom of Italy.

The region is fairly mountainous except for its eastern border, which is the magnificent coastline of the Adriatic. Less populated and economically prosperous than many regions of Italy, the area depends upon its crafts industry (articles produced in wrought iron, wood, pottery and wicker), fishing and tourism for its economy. The seaside resorts are busy for about six months of the year and the ports of Ancona and Pesaro have a fair amount of commercial activity and plenty of summer boat traffic to Croatia and Greece.

Urbino is the region's most interesting city. A little Renaissance jewel, it is the birthplace of Raphael. Loreto, however, is probably the most popular city of Marches, with approximately two million visitors a year. The attraction here is the Shrine of the Holy House. Legend has it that in 1295, when Muslims invaded the Holy Land, "angels" carried the family home of Jesus to Dalmatia and on to Italy in order to protect it. The three stone walls of the house are set in an elaborate chapel within the large Basilica of the Holy House, designed by Bramante in the sixteenth century. Research in the last few decades has confirmed that the stones are from the Middle East, and other markings on them suggest that they could well have come from the home of Jesus, Mary and Joseph in Nazareth. Further research indicates that the family of a thirteenth-century despot, Angeli, may have brought the house to Loreto.

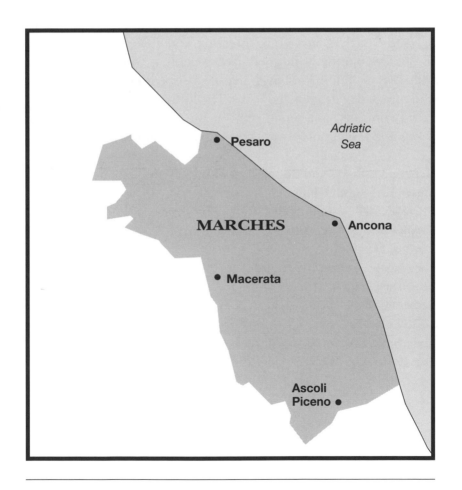

MARCHES

Pesaro

Adriatic
Sea

Ancona

Macerata

Ascoli
Piceno

Loreto

Casa del Clero Madonna di Loreto
Via Asdrubali, 104
Loreto 60025 (Ancona)
Tel. (071) 970 298 ▪ Fax (071) 750 0532

A beautiful, flower-filled courtyard forms an impressive entrance to Casa del Clero, a busy three-star hotel. The inside is as attractive as the outside, with good-sized reception rooms ornamented with flowers, fine furnishings, marble floors, a lovely dining room and updated bedrooms and baths. The location is marvelous—a few yards from the basilica and right in the old town, near charming shops and restaurants. A very hospitable guesthouse.

Rooms: 32 singles and doubles; all with bath and telephone.
Meals: Breakfast included.
Price: 55.000L (single); 85.000L (double).
Credit cards: Not accepted.
Curfew: Flexible.
Language(s) spoken: No English.
Facilities: Chapel.
Season: Open all year.
DIRECTIONS:
Train station: Ancona. Take local bus to Loreto.
Car: From A14 or SS Adriatica 16, follow signs to Loreto.

Casa di Accoglienza
Via Montereale Vecchio, 96
Loreto 60025 (Ancona)
Tel. (071) 970 192 ▪ Fax (071) 970 192

Behind beautiful iron gates in a quiet neighborhood, a few blocks from the basilica, the Ursuline sisters have a wonderful guesthouse. The public rooms are quite grand, with high ceilings and fine antique furnishings. Just beyond is a romantic, flower-filled terrace overlooking the exquisite Adriatic. The rooms upstairs are simple and several overlook the sea. This is an extremely hospitable and gracious house.

Rooms: 36 singles and doubles; most with bath.
Meals: Breakfast extra (3.500L); full board available upon request.
Price: 34.000L (single w/bath); 54.000L (double w/bath).
Credit cards: Not accepted.
Curfew: 11:45 P.M.
Language(s) spoken: Some English.
Facilities: Parking, elevator, TV room, chapel.
Season: Open all year except December 20–January 7.
DIRECTIONS:
Train station: Ancona. Take local bus to Loreto.
Car: From A14 or SS Adriatica 16, follow signs to Loreto.

Casa Francescana
Via Marconi, 26
Loreto 60025 (Ancona)
Tel. (071) 970 306

C asa Francescana is located on the busy main road leading to the center of Loreto. The house is small, plain and very clean. Although owned by an order of Franciscan sisters, the casa is run by a gracious lady who speaks no English but could not have been more helpful. The town and Shrine of Loreto are a fairly good walk, so wear comfortable shoes.

Rooms: 10 singles, doubles and triples; some with bath.
Meals: Breakfast extra (5.000L); full board available upon request.
Price: 25.000L–50.000L.
Credit cards: Not accepted.
Curfew: 10:00 P.M.
Language(s) spoken: No English.
Facilities: Chapel.
Season: Open all year.
DIRECTIONS:
Train station: Ancona. Take local bus to Loreto.
Car: From A14 or SS Adriatica 16, follow signs to Loreto.

Casa San Francesco
Via San Francesco, 15
Loreto 60025 (Ancona)
Tel. (071) 977 128 ▪ Fax (071) 978 237

L ocated some distance from the center of the old town, Casa San Francesco is designated a two-star hotel. A large monastery built around a pretty courtyard, it has four floors with many tiny, austere rooms. Ask for one facing the beautiful Adriatic. Fortunately, the lack of hospitality we experienced at this casa is not typical of Franciscan houses. However, if in great need of accommodations, it would be adequate.

Rooms: 79 singles and doubles; all with bath.
Meals: Breakfast extra (4.000L); full board available upon request.
Price: 55.000L (single); 70.000L (double).
Credit cards: Not accepted.
Curfew: Flexible.
Language(s) spoken: No English.
Facilities: Parking, elevator, TV room, conference facilities, restaurant, bar, chapel.
Season: Open all year.
DIRECTIONS:
Train station: Ancona. Take local bus to Loreto.
Car: Take A14 or SS Adriatica 16 and follow signs to Loreto.

Istituto S. Famiglia Piemonte
Via Asdrubali, 70
Loreto 60025 (Ancona)
Tel. (071) 977 685 ▪ Fax (071) 977 685

Behind an austere facade is a splendid guesthouse that has been designated a two-star hotel. The public rooms are inviting, with elegant marble floors throughout the entire building. While the bedrooms are plain, they are spotless, and the bathrooms are both modern and attractive. Centrally located in the heart of the old town, it is near the basilica, shops and restaurants. The gracious sister who took us through the house left us with an impression of a warm welcome for all.

Rooms: 45 singles and doubles; all with bath.
Meals: Breakfast included; full board available upon request.
Price: 40.000L (single); 56.000L (double).
Credit cards: Not accepted.
Curfew: 10:00 P.M.
Language(s) spoken: No English.
Facilities: Elevator, TV room, restaurant, bar, chapel.
Season: Open May–November.
DIRECTIONS:
Train station: Ancona. Take local bus to Loreto.
Car: From A14 or SS Adriatica 16, follow the signs to Loreto.

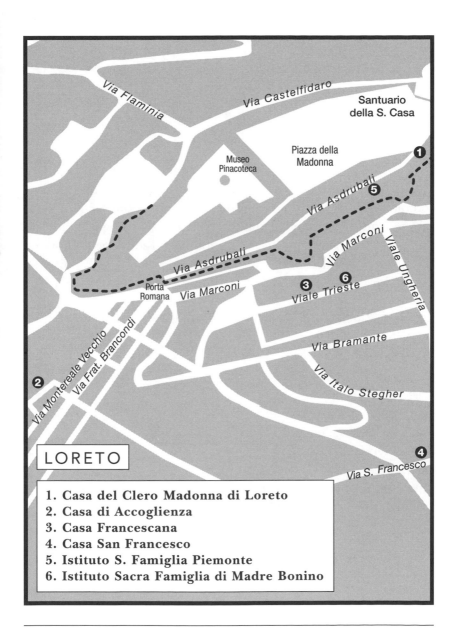

LORETO

1. Casa del Clero Madonna di Loreto
2. Casa di Accoglienza
3. Casa Francescana
4. Casa San Francesco
5. Istituto S. Famiglia Piemonte
6. Istituto Sacra Famiglia di Madre Bonino

Istituto Sacra Famiglia
di Madre Bonino
Via Trieste, 41
Loreto 60025 (Ancona)
Tel. (071) 977 133 ▪ Fax (071) 977 685

Directed by the Sisters of the Holy Family, this plain stone house is located on a quiet street in a residential and commercial area several blocks from the shrine. The accommodations are clean and simple, and most have balconies. The nuns are delightful and do their best to communicate with non-Italian-speaking visitors. A three-star hotel next door has a restaurant where meals could be taken, since none are served at this guesthouse.

Rooms: 13 singles and doubles; some with bath.
Meals: No meals.
Price: 35.000L per person.
Credit cards: Not accepted.
Curfew: 10:00 P.M.
Language(s) spoken: No English.
Facilities: Parking, elevator, TV room, chapel.
Season: Open all year.
DIRECTIONS:
Train station: Ancona. Take the bus to Loreto.
Car: From A14 or SS Adriatica 16, follow the signs to Loreto.

NOTES

PIEDMONT

Piedmont, a territory of mountains, valleys, lakes and rivers, is geographically one of the largest regions of Italy. Situated in the northwest, bordering France, the French influence on language, food and culture is quite evident. The area was inhabited before the first century B.C. by the Romans, later falling into the hands of the Lombards, Franks and, finally, the House of Savoy, which claimed title in 1230. The Kingdom of Sardinia took over in 1713, but by 1831 the agitation for Italian unification had started, with Turin as one of the main centers of the movement. When the Kingdom of Italy came into being, Turin was its first capital.

The economy of the region is excellent. The mainstay is the car industry, dominated by Fiat; agriculture (crops, including grapes for good regional wines), the textile industry and tourism add to Piedmont's prosperity.

Lake Maggiore is perhaps one of the main destinations for tourists. North of Milan, nestled against the Alps, it is a spectacular body of water surrounded by charming little towns and elegant villas.

Cannobio, just three kilometers from the Swiss border, is a charming little town that has been in existence for more than a thousand years. A beautiful waterfront with colorful sixteenth- and seventeenth-century houses on the promenade, tiny boutiques offering expensive clothes and crafts, good restaurants, a festive Sunday market and excellent climate all entice visitors.

Verbania-Intra is a bustling old town on the western side of the lake. Old churches and ruins abound; hiking, fishing, swimming, sailing and windsurfing are available for visitors; a great Saturday market is held on a main street and the ferry terminal offers boat service to all parts of the lake, including Switzerland.

Stresa, the major resort on the lake, is a jewel of cobblestone streets, flowers and palms, pretty, colorful houses, festive cafes and marvelous climate. The famous—Toscanini, Wagner, Hemingway and Goethe, among others—and the not so famous, have long been drawn to this idyllic town. A wonderful music festival is held here every year in mid-August, and the elegant Borromean Islands are just a quick boat trip away.

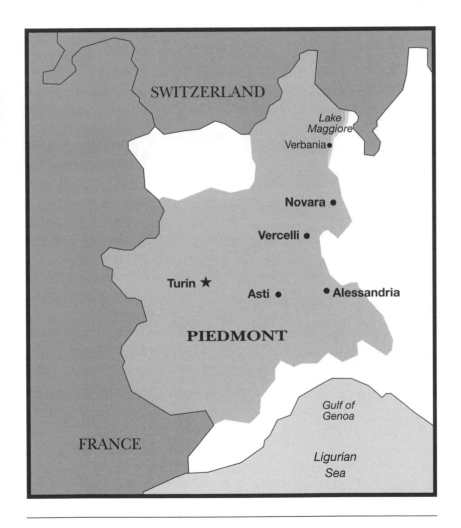

Cannobio

Hotel Il Portico
Piazza Santuario
Cannobio 28052 (Verbania)
Tel. (0323) 712 55/705 98 ▪ Fax (0323) 722 89

Located on the banks of Lake Maggiore, Il Portico is owned and operated by the Diocese of Novara. This small, modern, three-star hotel has pretty rooms with tiled floors, nice public rooms, a dining room with vaulted ceilings and a lovely garden. It is adjacent to the S. S. Pieta Sanctuary and within easy walking distance of the shops and restaurants in this charming and sophisticated town of Cannobio. The Swiss border is less than three miles away.

Rooms: 38 singles and doubles; all with bath and telephone.
Meals: Breakfast extra (10.000L).
Price: 75.000L (single); 120.000L (double).
Credit cards: All major.
Curfew: No.
Language(s) spoken: Some English.
Facilities: Parking, elevator, TV room, meeting rooms, restaurant, bar.
Season: Open all year.
DIRECTIONS:
Train station: Stresa or Baveno. Then take a bus to Cannobio.
Car: From Milan, take A8 north, exit Arona-Stresa exit and continue north on SS 34 to Cannobio (approximately 65 kilometers).

Stresa

Collegio Rosmini
Via Manzoni, 10
Stresa 28049 (Verbania)
Tel. (0323) 311 89/313 72 ▪ Fax (0323) 336 71

Collegio Rosmini is at the end of a long cobblestone, palm-tree-lined driveway high on a hill above Lake Maggiore. The large monastery has incredible views of Stresa, the Borromeo Islands and the mountains beyond. Since it is a school, the rooms are plain and simple, but many have balconies overlooking the garden and lake. The accommodations are primarily geared toward groups, but individuals are welcome if there is room. The priest in charge speaks English and is most helpful and quite funny—a welcome relief if your Italian is not up to speed.

Rooms: Singles and doubles; a few with bath.
Meals: Breakfast included; full board available upon request.
Price: 35.000L per person.
Credit cards: Not accepted.
Curfew: 11:00 P.M.
Language(s) spoken: English.
Facilities: Parking, TV room, tennis, chapel.
Season: Open all year.
DIRECTIONS:
Train station: Stresa. Take a taxi.
Car: From A26 north, exit Carpungineno-Stresa. About five minutes before arriving in Stresa, make a right turn into the property—a small sign is on the left side of the road just before the turn.

Verbania-Intra

Hotel Il Chiostro
Via Fratelli Cervi, 14
Verbania-Intra 28044 (Verbania)
Tel. (0323) 404 077 ▪ Fax (0323) 401 231

For many centuries the home of Augustinian nuns, this cloister has been restored and expanded to its present status as a three-star hotel. The newer part has small, modern rooms, many of which overlook the beautiful enclosed garden with its ancient well. The older section contains a chapel, simple sitting and meeting rooms and part of the restaurant, all of which have the cloister's original ceilings, walls and floors. The location is a short walk from the lake and bustling town center. If you're in town for a weekend, visit the Saturday market; it is small but terrific.

Rooms: 70 singles and doubles; all with bath, telephone and TV.
Meals: Breakfast included; full board available upon request.
Price: 65.000L–90.000L (single); 100.000L–140.000L (double).
Credit cards: All major.
Curfew: 12:00 A.M.
Language(s) spoken: English, French, German.
Facilities: Parking, elevator, TV rooms, meeting rooms, restaurant, bar, library, tennis courts, auditorium, chapel.
Season: Open all year.
DIRECTIONS:
Train station: Verbania. Take a taxi.
Car: From A26 north, exit Carpungnino Stresa and continue north on SS 34 to Verbania Intra.

NOTES

SICILY

L and of mafia and mythology, Sicily, the largest island in the Mediterranean, is a crossroads of civilizations: archaeological findings date from the Stone Age, after which Phoenicians, Greeks, Romans, Arabs, Saracens, French and Spanish left their mark here until 1860, when Garibaldi liberated the region. Shortly thereafter the populace, by plebiscite, chose to become part of the Kingdom of Italy. The capital, Palermo, could be beautiful, with its broad streets, elegant, expensive shops, impressive art and architecture from past conquerors; instead it is frenetic, polluted, congested and noisy.

The economy is poorly developed and, as a result, high crime and unemployment rates are evident in many areas. The mainstays are agriculture, fishing, a small petrochemical sector (which has caused pollution in some places) and tourism. There is a great deal to do and see on this ancient island despite the fact that it is not as tourist-oriented as northern Italy. The following towns have religious houses of hospitality.

Santa Martino delle Scale, not too far from Palermo, has been a religious settlement since the sixth century. The small village has become a summer resort in recent years but retains its charm and peacefulness. Close by is Monreale, an old hill town with a famous Norman church housing spectacular medieval mosaics and an unusually pretty cloister.

Siculiana Marina is a small, undistinguished village; the big attraction is the nearby "Valley of the Temples" on the outskirts of Agrigento. Dating from the sixth century B.C., the Greek temples are in various stages of restoration, but that does not detract from the awesome sight and setting.

Siracusa, founded by Corinthians about 735 B.C., once rivaled Athens in wealth and power. At its heart is the little ancient island of Ortigia, where brightly painted eighteenth- and nineteenth-century houses decorate the harbor and the Piazza del Duomo, which is anchored by a grandiose cathedral built over a fifth-century B.C. temple of Minerva (some of whose original Doric columns are still visible). Beyond the island there is a fine archaeological park that contains Greek and Roman ruins. Nearby there are catacombs where Saints Peter and Paul once preached.

Noto was totally destroyed in 1693 by a horrendous earthquake. Almost immediately, the people rebuilt the city with elegant honey-colored baroque buildings and large plazas adorned with tropical plantings. Over time the city deteriorated badly; however, since 1987 a slow but massive restoration has begun.

Viagrande is a small, uninteresting town. However, its proximity to historical towns and to Taormina, a glitzy, fashionable resort high above the Ionian Sea, makes it a practical and enjoyable stop.

Zafferna Etnea is a delightful little village on the slopes of Mount Etna. Lovely views of the blue Mediterranean, quaint shops and cafes and hospitable townspeople will enhance a visit.

Noto

Casa di Accoglienza
Santa Maria Scala del Paradiso
Contrada Scala
Noto 96017 (Siracusa)
Tel. (0931) 894 013

Built adjacent to Noto Antica, which until 1693 was an important city of Sicily, this convent was established around the same time, destroyed in 1715 and subsequently rebuilt. Today's inhabitants operate a house of hospitality, and have managed to update the structure while retaining its charm and panoramic views. The approach to this convent is a spectacular ride through rolling hills of lush orange groves and magnificent scenery. Shortly before coming to the entrance, the Stations of the Cross appear in beautiful little shrines on both sides of the road.

Rooms: Singles and doubles; some with bath.
Meals: Breakfast included; full board available upon request.
Price: 40.000L–50.000L per person.
Credit cards: Not accepted.
Curfew: Flexible.
Language(s) spoken: No English.
Facilities: Parking, meeting rooms, garden and chapel.
Season: April–October.
DIRECTIONS:
Car: From Siracusa take SS 115 toward Noto; turn north (right) on SS 287 and follow the signs for approximately sixteen kilometers.

Monastero San Benedetto
Via dei Mille, 106/108
Noto 96017 (Siracusa)
Tel. (0931) 891 2255 ▪ Fax (0931) 894 382

*C*onstructed in the seventeenth century, this Benedictine monastery is an elegant building set in a beautiful tropical garden. It is about thirty-three kilometers from Siracusa in Noto, a town famous for its splendid baroque buildings. The monastery was under restoration at the time of our visit, but the Mother Prioress (Madre Priora M. M. Deletta Lantieri) will quickly respond to a fax requesting information. Be sure to send it in Italian.

Rooms: 13 singles and doubles; most with bath.
Meals: Breakfast included; half and full board available upon request.
Price: 30.000L–50.000L per person.
Credit cards: Not accepted.
Curfew: Flexible.
Language(s) spoken: No English.
Facilities: Parking, TV room, garden and chapel.
Season: Open all year except Easter and Christmas.
DIRECTIONS:
Train station: Noto. Take a taxi.
Car: SS 115 from Siracusa to Noto, then follow signs to the monastery.

San Martino delle Scale

Abbazia Benedettini

Piazza ai Platani, 11

San Martino delle Scale 90040 (Palermo)

Tel. (091) 418 104 ▪ Fax (091) 418 104

In the hills high above Palermo sits this Benedictine abbey, which was founded in the late sixth century by Gregory the Great, destroyed in 830 and rebuilt in 1347. The long, narrow, winding road leading to it offers spectacular vistas of the sea and the magnificent Sicilian countryside. The old buildings and grounds are in need of refurbishing, but the rooms are clean and adequate, and several good works of art are housed in the sprawling complex. A school and vineyards are on the property, and wine and other products the monks produce are sold at the abbey.

Rooms: 41 singles and doubles; half with bath.
Meals: Full board only.
Price: 50.000L per person.
Credit cards: Not accepted.
Curfew: No.
Language(s) spoken: No English.
Facilities: Parking, chapel.
Season: Open all year.
DIRECTIONS:
Bus: From Palermo buses run from Piazza Giuseppe to San Martino delle Scale.
Car: From Palermo drive to Monreale; follow signs to the abbey.

Siculiana Marina

Casa dell'Accoglienza Don Giustino
Via Principe di Piemonte, 1
Siculiana Marina 92010 (Agrigento)
Tel. (0922) 815 210 ▪ Fax (0922) 817 484

In a peaceful setting of pine trees and gray cliffs is Casa Don Giustino. The buildings and accommodations are clean and very plain. The location, however, is near the water and there are many good sandy beaches. The most important attraction in the area is in Agrigento, twelve miles to the east. There one can view the spectacular "Valley of the Temples," built in the fifth century B.C. The six temples are some of the best-preserved Greek architecture in the world. It is a sight not to be missed, particularly at sunset.

Rooms: 28 singles and doubles; all with bath.
Meals: Half or full board only.
Price: 50.000L (half board); 65.000L (full board) per person.
Credit cards: Not accepted.
Curfew: Flexible.
Language(s) spoken: No English.
Facilities: Parking, elevator, TV room, conference facilities, chapel.
Season: Open all year except July and August.
DIRECTIONS:
Car: From Agrigento head west on highway 115, about 18 kilometers.

Siracusa

Albergo Domus Mariae
Via Vittorio Veneto, 76
Siracusa 96100 (Siracusa)
Tel. (0931) 248 54 ▪ Fax (0931) 248 58

In the early light of dawn beneath the windows of Domus Mariae, fishermen can be seen perched on rocks, casting lines into the sea, as their forebears have done for over two thousand years on the shores of Ortigia Island. Situated in ancient Siracusa, this three-star hotel is a little gem owned by Ursuline sisters. The old palazzo was completely renovated in 1995 with extensive use of marble, good lighting and modern bathrooms. The sea views from some of the rooms are incredible. Across the street is an old church with exquisite mosaic floors; nearby is the Piazza del Duomo, with small boutiques and lively cafes, and just beyond is the historic port of Siracusa.

Rooms: 18 singles and doubles; all with bath, telephone and TV.
Meals: Breakfast included.
Price: 140.000L (single); 180.000L (double).
Credit cards: All major.
Curfew: No.
Language(s) spoken: Some English.
Facilities: Parking, conference facilities, air conditioning, restaurant, bar, chapel.
Season: Open all year.
DIRECTIONS:
Car: From SS 114 go through Siracusa, following signs to Ortigia; after crossing the bridge, turn left to the water; take a right; Via V. Veneto is straight ahead.

Viagrande

Madonna Degli Ulivi
Via Umberto, 266
Viagrande 95029 (Catania)
Tel. (095) 789 4177 ▪ Fax (095) 789 5570

Above the small town of Viagrande, "Madonna of the Olives" sits on the lower slopes of Mount Etna. Most of the well-equipped rooms are in small bungalows spread throughout the vast parklike grounds planted with flowers, shrubs and large trees. Besides the many recreational facilities on the premises, there are numerous hiking trails in the area. Easy day trips to Catania, Siracusa, Taormina and Agrigento are also possible.

Rooms: 70 singles, doubles and triples; all with bath, telephone, TV and air conditioning.
Meals: Breakfast included; half and full board available upon request.
Price: 65.000L (single); 108.000L (double).
Credit cards: Not accepted.
Curfew: No.
Language(s) spoken: No English.
Facilities: Parking, conference facilities, restaurant, bar, swimming pool, tennis, other sports facilities, chapel.
Season: Open all year.
DIRECTIONS:
Train station: Acireale. Take a taxi.
Car: A18, exit S. Gregorio-Acireale, follow signs to Viagrande, continue through the town, watch for signs—it is on the right.

Zafferana Etnea

Albergo del Bosco Emmaus
Via Cassone, 75
Zafferana Etnea 95019 (Catania)
Tel. (095) 708 1888/708 1910 ▪ Fax (095) 708 3824

Located on the lower slopes of Mount Etna, Albergo del Bosco is an ideal stop when touring Sicily. While the building itself is a large, unattractive concrete structure, the simple rooms (many with balconies) offer incredible views of the snow-covered volcano, vineyards and orchards or the blue Mediterranean. This wonderful location is a short drive from the charming town of Zafferana Etnea, with its cute shops and cafes, and not far from Catania and Taormina. Easy day trips to historical Agrigento and Siracusa are possible. The ski areas are close by and excellent hiking trails are open during most of the year.

Rooms: 87 singles, doubles and triples; all with bath.
Meals: Half and full board only.
Price: 65.000L (half board) per person; 100.000L (full board) per person. (Prices lower for children.)
Credit cards: Not accepted.
Curfew: No.
Language(s) spoken: No English.
Facilities: Parking, elevator, TV room, conference facilities, restaurant, bar, chapel.
Season: Open all year.
DIRECTIONS:
Car: A18 between Catania and Taormina, exit Giarre. Pass through Zafferana; follow signs to Emmaus.

NOTES

TUSCANY

Rolling hills, gentle valleys, magnificent forests, peaceful rivers and nature at its very best define the attributes of this region in the heart of Italy. Starting with the Etruscans, from whom the region's name is derived, the citizens of Tuscany have been invaded by Gauls, Romans and hordes of barbarians, among others. From the eleventh to the fifteenth centuries, Tuscany was a group of independent city-states; the Medicis amassed power toward the end of that period and held it until the eighteenth century. Finally, in 1860, Tuscany became part of the Kingdom of Italy.

The economy of the region is quite prosperous, with light industry, crafts, food, wine and, especially, tourism forming the basis. There are many convents in the region.

Cortona is not a frequent stop for tourists, but it is well worth a visit. Inhabited by the Etruscans around the eighth century B.C., it is one of the oldest hill towns in Italy. The little city contains two fine museums that history buffs would enjoy, a bustling town center and incredible views of the luxuriant, rolling hills.

Fiesole is a delightful village in the Tuscan hills. Day trippers from Florence come often to visit the extensive Etruscan ruins, the remains of a first-century B.C. Roman theater and many other old, interesting sights. Festive cafes and restaurants, quaint shops and an incredible view of the city of Florence, dominated by its red-roofed duomo, add to the charm.

Florence, the birthplace and heart of the Renaissance, must be experienced to be believed. The duomo, baptistry, Santa Maria Novella, Santa Croce, Medici Chapels, Accademia, Pitti Palace and Uffizi are some of the major attractions. But almost every nook and cranny of "Centro Storico" holds a wonderful gem of history. The shopping runs the gamut from elegant and pricey to boisterous, bargain-filled open-air markets. The restaurants and cafes offer a profusion of wonderful Tuscan food and good local wines. Whatever your age, interests or price range, Florence will have something for you.

San Gimignano, a charming Tuscan hill town, still has fifteen of the original seventy-two towers built around the fourteenth century for both defense and prestige. The picturesque medieval enclave, with its churches, museums and shops on narrow streets and squares, is an interesting stop. The city fathers have even seen fit to open a Museum of Torture, with documents and instruments from the Inquisition!

Once one of the most important cities of Europe, Siena is the home of Saint Catherine, Italy's patron saint. A magnificent zebra-striped duomo and the Piazza del Campo (site of the famous Palio) are among the many other worthwhile attractions. Fun cafes, good ice cream and sophisticated shops will add to the visitor's enjoyment.

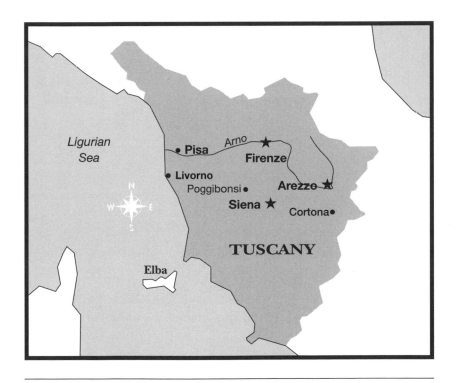

Camaldoli

Foresteria del Monastero di Camaldoli
Via Camaldoli
Camaldoli 52010 (Arezzo)
Tel. (0575) 556 013 ▪ Fax (0575) 556 001

For hundreds of years, Benedictine monks have worked and prayed in the forested hills of Tuscany. Part of their mission at Camaldoli has included hospitality for retreatants and visitors. Accommodations are simple, the public rooms quite large and the spectacular library, dating from 1620, has over thirty thousand volumes. The grounds are extensive, with many paths through the woods; the church and chapels contain beautiful works of art, and there is a shop where the monks sell their products: wine, honey, cosmetics and many other outstanding items.

Rooms: 90 singles, doubles and triples; half with bath.
Meals: Half or full board only.
Price: 65.000L (half board); 75.000L (full board) per person.
Credit cards: Not accepted.
Curfew: Flexible.
Language(s) spoken: English.
Facilities: Parking, elevator, TV room, meeting rooms, library, chapel.
Season: Easter–September.
DIRECTIONS:
Train station: Bibbiera. Take a taxi or the Camaldoli bus.
Car: A1, exit Arezzo, north on roadway no. 71 to Bibbiera, then take local road to Camaldoli (approximately 4 kilometers).

Cortona

Albergo Oasi Giovanni Neumann

Via delle Contesse, 1

Cortona 52044 (Arezzo)

Tel. (0575) 630 127 ▪ Fax (0575) 630 354

S et on a picturesque slope outside the walled city of Cortona a congregation of Redemptorists direct a three-star hotel for guests who wish to vacation or make a spiritual retreat. This typical Tuscan house has fine, comfortable accommodations (many with views of the vineyards and olive groves), a wonderful garden and good food. The location is excellent for touring the spectacular countryside.

Rooms: 44 singles, doubles and triples; most with bath.
Meals: Breakfast extra (10.000L).
Price: 75.000L (single); 130.000L (double).
Credit cards: Not accepted.
Curfew: Flexible.
Language(s) spoken: Some English.
Facilities: Parking, elevator, 2 TV rooms, restaurant, bar, chapel.
Season: Open all year.
DIRECTIONS:
Train or bus station: Camucia. Take a taxi or call beforehand to arrange for them to pick you up for a small fee.

Casa Betania
Via Gino Severini, 50
Cortona 52044 (Arezzo)
Tel. (0575) 628 29

Just outside the walls of this ancient Tuscan hill town reputed to have existed since 1000 B.C., the sisters at Casa Betania offer plain, clean accommodations and plenty of good food. The location is excellent for enjoying this wonderful walled city of Etruscan, Roman and medieval art and sweeping panoramas of Lake Trasimeno and the rolling hills of Tuscany.

Rooms: 31 singles, doubles and triples; half with bath.
Meals: Full board only.
Price: 65.000L per person.
Credit cards: Not accepted.
Curfew: No.
Language(s) spoken: No English.
Facilities: Chapel.
Season: Open all year except September 10–20.
DIRECTIONS:
Train/bus station: Carmucia. Take local bus; ask for "Casa Betania" stop.
Car: From Camucia head straight up toward the town; at first cross-roads turn right and continue on, watching for signs: "Casa Betania."

Istituto Santa Margherita

Via Cesare Battisti, 15

Cortona 52044 (Arezzo)

Tel. (0575) 630 336 ▪ Fax (0575) 630 549

The Istituto Santa Margherita boasts a splendid location on the local bus line and within walking distance of the historic town center. A simple foyer contains lovely antiques, and, while most of the rooms are plain and comfortable, room no. 17, near the entrance, is particularly charming, with large double doors, a high ceiling and a grand chandelier. The sisters are very hospitable and will provide guests with keys so they can come and go as they please in this fascinating town.

Rooms: 20 singles, doubles and triples; most with bath.
Meals: Breakfast included.
Price: 38.000L (single); 66.000L (double); 84.000L (triple).
Credit cards: Not accepted.
Curfew: No.
Language(s) spoken: No English.
Facilities: Elevator, meeting rooms, chapel.
Season: Open all year.
DIRECTIONS:
Train/bus station: Camucia. Take bus to Piazza Garibaldi, just outside the city walls. Walk down the Via Gino Severini to Viale C. Battisti.

Monastero della S. S. Trinita
Via San Nicolo, 2
Cortona 52044 (Arezzo)
Tel. (0575) 603 345

This old stone monastery built in 1268 was closed at the time of our visit. It is our understanding, however, that the Cistercians provide very basic, clean, safe accommodations in this house. We included it as a possible prospect because it is located within the walled city of narrow cobblestone streets, interesting churches, historic artifacts, good restaurants, lively cafes and small boutiques.

Rooms: 15 singles, doubles and triples; half with bath.
Meals: None.
Price: 25.000L per person.
Credit cards: Not accepted.
Curfew: Flexible.
Language(s) spoken: No English.
Facilities: Elevator, chapel.
Season: Open May–October.
DIRECTIONS:
Train/bus station: Camucia. Take local bus to Via San Nicolo.
Car: From Perugia, exit Cortona and follow signs to "Centro."

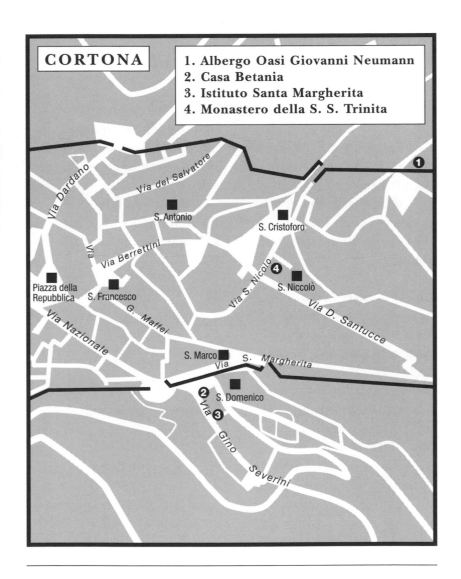

CORTONA

1. Albergo Oasi Giovanni Neumann
2. Casa Betania
3. Istituto Santa Margherita
4. Monastero della S. S. Trinita

Via Dardano

Via del Salvatore

S. Antonio

S. Cristoforo

Via Berrettini

Via

Via S. Nicolo

❹

S. Niccolò

Piazza della
Repubblica

S. Francesco

Via D. Santucce

Via Nazionale

G. Maffei

S. Marco

Via S. Margherita

❷ S. Domenico

❸

Via

Gino

Severini

❶

Florence

Istituto Santa Zita
Via Nazionale, 8
Florence 50123 (Firenze)
Tel. (055) 239 8202

The Sisters of the Holy Spirit offer hospitality to summer visitors at their home in the heart of Florence. The accommodations are located on the upper floors of an old, austere building. One must enter through large wooden doors to a dismal garage-like first floor, then take an ancient elevator cage to the clean, comfortable and plain rooms above. While lacking the eye-pleasing beauty of many other convents, this one offers the convenience of location: two blocks from the train station and within walking distance of all the historic sites.

Rooms: Doubles and triples; all with bath.
Meals: Breakfast included.
Price: 40,000L per person.
Credit cards: Not accepted.
Curfew: 11:00 P.M.
Language(s) spoken: No English.
Season: July, August and September (for single women and families).
DIRECTIONS:
Train station: Santa Maria Novella. Walk to Piazza della Stazione. Via Nazionale runs into the plaza.

Casa Regina del Santo Rosario

Via Giusti, 35

Florence 50121 (Firenze)

Tel. (055) 247 7636/247 7650

L ocated a few blocks from the Accademia, the street on which this convent is located is not particularly good; however, the adjacent neighborhood is quite lovely and the location is excellent for touring Florence. Open to women only, the kind and hospitable sisters offer safe, comfortable accommodations in a pleasant house.

Rooms: 20 singles and doubles (for women only); 10 with bath.
Meals: Breakfast included; half board available upon request.
Price: 35.000L–40.000L per person.
Credit cards: Not accepted.
Curfew: 11:00 P.M.
Language(s) spoken: No English.
Facilities: TV room, chapel.
Season: Open July–September.
DIRECTIONS:
Train station: Santa Maria Novella. Take bus no. 3 or 32 to Colonna and Borgo Pinti—V. Giusti is two blocks north.

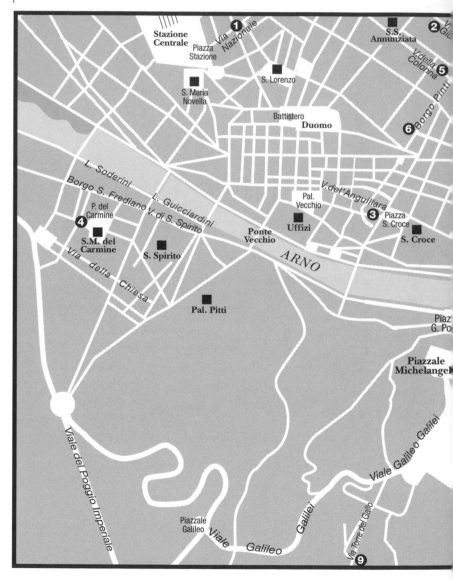

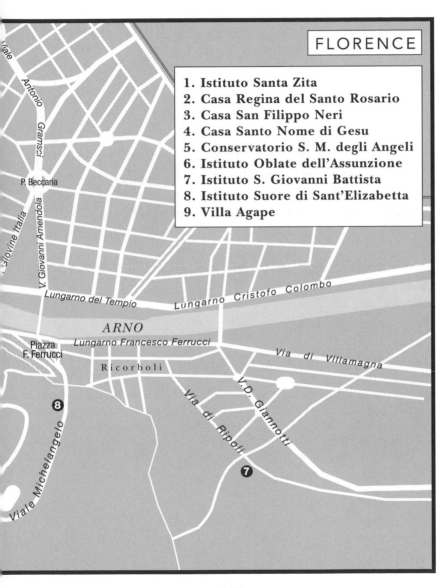

FLORENCE

1. Istituto Santa Zita
2. Casa Regina del Santo Rosario
3. Casa San Filippo Neri
4. Casa Santo Nome di Gesu
5. Conservatorio S. M. degli Angeli
6. Istituto Oblate dell'Assunzione
7. Istituto S. Giovanni Battista
8. Istituto Suore di Sant'Elizabetta
9. Villa Agape

Casa San Filippo Neri

Via dell'Anguillara, 25

Florence 50122 (Firenze)

Tel. (055) 211 331/214 166

G uests are housed on a separate floor of this building, which is home to both priests and students. While the baths are updated and sparkling, the halls and bedrooms are desperate for a makeover. The casa is best suited for students but is included because of its fantastic location—in the heart of historical Florence, quite close to the Uffizi, the duomo, and just down the street from Santa Croce, burial place of Michelangelo, Galileo and Machiavelli, among others.

Rooms: 13 singles and doubles; none with bath.
Meals: No meals.
Price: 30.000L per person.
Credit cards: Not accepted.
Curfew: No.
Language(s) spoken: Some English, French.
Facilities: TV room.
Season: Open summer only.
DIRECTIONS:
Train station: Santa Maria Novella. Take a taxi or bus no. 14; get off at Ghibellina and walk two blocks toward the Arno.

Casa Santo Nome di Gesu
Piazza del Carmine, 21
Florence 50124 (Firenze)
Tel. (055) 213 856/214 866 ▪ Fax (055) 281 835

In a lively Florentine district not far from the Arno, large, simple doors open on to a convent filled with exquisite antiques and bustling nuns (the mother superior does not make a move without her cell phone in hand). Daylight streams through a skylight onto an elegant eighteenth-century staircase that leads to spotless, high-ceilinged guest rooms offering garden or piazza views. Carved mahogany beds covered in pretty floral prints rest on terra-cotta floors. The windows are covered by large wooden shutters. The library and meeting rooms are both functional and richly decorated.

Rooms: 22 singles, doubles and triples; none with bath.
Meals: Breakfast included; half board available upon request.
Price: 55.000L per person.
Credit cards: Not accepted.
Curfew: 10:30 P.M. winter/11:30 P.M. summer.
Language(s) spoken: Some English, French.
Facilities: Parking, TV room, meeting rooms, library, chapel.
Season: Open all year except August 15–September 1.
DIRECTIONS:
Train station: Santa Maria Novella. Take a taxi or bus no. 6, 11, 35 or 36b to Piazza di Carmine.

Conservatorio S. M. degli Angeli
Via della Colonna, 34
Florence 50121 (Firenze)
Tel. (055) 247 8051

Since 1507 this beautiful monastery has existed in the heart of Florence. Built around a flower-filled cloister, the main rooms are elegant, with high, vaulted ceilings, terra cotta tiled floors, a profusion of plants and wonderful religious art, including a magnificent fresco of the Last Supper by Matteo Rosselli in the dining room. The upstairs rooms are quite comfortable, and several open on to the upper terrace. Located close to all the wonders of Florence, the graciousness of the sisters will only enhance your stay.

Rooms: 59 singles and doubles; some with bath.
Meals: Breakfast included; half and full board available upon request.
Price: 50.000L–59.000L per person.
Credit cards: Not accepted.
Curfew: 1:00 A.M.
Language(s) spoken: No English.
Facilities: TV room, meeting rooms, chapel.
Season: Open July–September.
DIRECTIONS:
Train station: Santa Maria Novella. Take bus no. 31 or 32 to M. Archeologico.

Istituto Oblate dell'Assunzione
Borgo Pinti, 15
Florence 50121 (Firenze)
Tel. (055) 248 0582/3 ▪ Fax (055) 234 6291

A drab facade on a busy street hides a wonderful surprise. Inside, delightful, hospitable sisters run a fantastic guesthouse in a former Florentine villa. Exquisite antiques and religious art are scattered throughout; high, vaulted ceilings, frescoed walls and terracotta floors are reminiscent of a different time, while the comfortable accommodations and pretty tiled baths are as modern as can be. The spacious garden is an enchanting oasis in this marvelous, bustling city.

Rooms: 30 singles, doubles and triples; some with bath.
Meals: Board available upon request.
Price: 45.000L per person.
Credit cards: Not accepted.
Curfew: 11:00 P.M.
Language(s) spoken: Some English.
Facilities: Elevator, TV room, meeting rooms, chapel.
Season: Open all year.
DIRECTIONS:
Train station: Santa Maria Novella. Take a taxi with luggage; otherwise it's easier to walk.

Istituto S. Giovanni Battista
Via Ripoli, 82
Florence 50126 (Firenze)
Tel. (055) 680 2394

Situated some distance from the center of Florence, the Battistina sisters have a large Italian villa in a modest residential area. The house is surrounded by gray stone walls, within which are extensive gardens planted with tropical trees, shrubs and flowers. The public rooms are baroque, elegantly painted and furnished with exceptional antiques complemented by an abundance of greenery. The accommodations are simple yet extremely comfortable.

Rooms: 11 singles and doubles; all with bath.
Meals: Breakfast included; half board available upon request.
Price: 60.000L (single); 100.000L (double).
Credit cards: Not accepted.
Curfew: Flexible.
Language(s) spoken: No English.
Facilities: Parking.
Season: Open all year.
DIRECTIONS:
Train station: Santa Maria Novella. Take bus no. 31 or 32.

Istituto Suore di Sant'Elizabetta
Viale Michelangelo, 46
Florence 50125 (Firenze)
Tel. (055) 681 1884

This elegant villa, just outside the city center is nestled in a residential neighborhood of palatial homes. At the top of this street is the Piazzale Michelangelo, where one can enjoy stunning views of Florence and magnificent sunsets that are not to be missed. The nuns of Saint Elizabeth are very kind and have a tremendous sense of humor. The rooms are small but immaculate, and the bathrooms are as good as any you will find in a hotel. The main corridors, highlighted by skylights and impressive stained-glass windows, are covered in a brown and white mosaic tile and adorned with antiques. A nice breakfast room where tables are covered in white linen overlooks a graceful garden. This is the perfect place for those looking for peace and quiet.

Rooms: 35 singles, doubles and triples; some with bath.
Meals: Breakfast included.
Price: 45.000L per person.
Credit cards: Not accepted.
Curfew: 10:00 P.M.
Language(s) spoken: Some English, German, Polish.
Facilities: Parking, TV room, meeting room, chapel.
Season: Open all year.
DIRECTIONS:
Train station: Santa Maria Novella. Take a taxi or bus no. 13, 23 or 33 to Piazza Ferucci, then walk up Viale Michelangelo.

Oasi Sacro Cuore
Via della Piazzola, 4
Florence 50133 (Firenze)
Tel. (055) 577 588/574 662

A quick bus ride from the historic center brings you to this comfortable house in a nice Florentine neighborhood. This pleasant establishment is open to tourists and groups, and the sisters provide good accommodations, a large meeting room and a colorful garden. This is a good choice for those who wish to avoid the commotion of the city, yet be close for sight-seeing.

Rooms: 24 singles, doubles and triples; most with bath.
Meals: Breakfast included; half and full board available upon request.
Price: 50.000L per person.
Credit cards: Not accepted.
Curfew: 11:00 P.M.
Language(s) spoken: No English.
Facilities: TV room, meeting rooms, chapel.
Season: Open all year.
DIRECTIONS:
Train station: Santa Maria Novella. Take bus no. 7, 11, 17 or 20 to Pacinotti.

Villa Agape
Via Torre del Gallo, 8/10
Florence 50125 (Firenze)
Tel. (055) 220 044 ■ Fax (055) 233 7012

Wide, tree-lined streets lead the way to this fine guesthouse set in a neighborhood of elegant private villas. The sisters provide good food, comfortable accommodations and a beautiful garden. High in the hills above Florence, Villa Agape is a wonderful place for rest and relaxation after a busy day of sight-seeing.

Rooms: 30 singles, doubles and triples; all with bath.
Meals: Breakfast included.
Price: 70.000L (single); 130.000L (double).
Credit cards: Not accepted.
Curfew: 10:30 P.M.
Language(s) spoken: No English.
Facilities: Parking, TV room, meeting rooms, chapel.
Season: Open all year.
DIRECTIONS:
Train station: Santa Maria Novella. Take bus no. 36 or 37 to Porta Romana and transfer to bus no. 12. Get off at the second stop on Viale Michelangelo, cross the street to Via Giramontino and follow signs to the villa.

Villa I Cancelli
Via Incontri, 21
Florence 50139 (Firenze)
Tel. (055) 422 6001 ■ Fax (055) 422 6001

A few miles from the hustle and bustle of Florence, Ursuline sisters graciously welcome guests to their lovely Italian villa. Surrounded by beautifully landscaped formal gardens in a picturesque district, this peaceful retreat offers attractive public rooms and comfortable accommodations located on the villa's first floor.

Rooms: 31 singles and doubles; most with bath.
Meals: Breakfast included.
Price: 75.000L (single); 140.000L (double).
Credit cards: Not accepted.
Curfew: 10:00 P.M.
Language(s) spoken: No English.
Facilities: Parking, meeting rooms, chapel.
Season: Open all year.
DIRECTIONS:
Train station: Santa Maria Novella. Take a taxi or city bus no. 14C; then transfer to bus 40 A or B.

Villa Linda

Via Poggi Gherardo, 5
Florence 50135 (Firenze)
Tel. (055) 603 913/617 000

In the rolling hills of Tuscany, not far from the center of Florence, charming Benedictine sisters oversee an elegant sixteenth-century villa. The walkways in front of the two-story stucco house are dotted with terra-cotta pots overflowing with brilliant flowers. Inside, the main drawing room has a lovely frescoed ceiling from which is suspended a large Venetian glass chandelier. The dining room is bright and cheerful, the sparkling clean rooms are quite comfortable, many offering good views of the picturesque pine-covered hills.

Rooms: 10 singles, doubles and triples; some with bath.
Meals: Breakfast included.
Price: 45.000L per person.
Credit cards: Not accepted.
Curfew: 11:00 P.M.
Language(s) spoken: English, French.
Facilities: Parking, TV room, meeting rooms, chapel.
Season: Open all year.
DIRECTIONS:
Train station: Santa Maria Novella. Take a taxi or bus no. 10. Stop at Ponte Amenzola.

La Verna

Santuario della Verna

Chiusi della Verna

La Verna 52010 (Arezzo)

Tel. (0575) 5341/534 211 ▪ Fax (0575) 599 320

Farewell! I depart from you in my person, but my heart I leave with you. . . ." Speaking these words to his friars, Saint Francis of Assisi took final leave of his beloved La Verna, the sacred monastery where he received the stigmata of Christ. Built under his direction between 1214 and 1224, the oldest structures tower a thousand meters above the Casentino Valley, just north of Arezzo. Several chapels and holy places contain exquisite frescoes and incredible Della Robbias, probably the finest collection anywhere. Today, ancient passageways and a multitude of stairwells lead to clean, comfortable guest rooms.

Tranquility is the best word to describe this glorious monastery, which will delight those who love the outdoors or those who desire complete rest and relaxation. The road to La Verna is long and winding, and as there are no lights, it is advisable to arrive before dark.

Rooms: 62 singles, doubles and triples; all with bath.
Meals: Half and full board available upon request.
Price: 40.000L (single); 50.000L (double); 60.000L (triple).
Credit cards: Not accepted.
Curfew: Flexible.
Language(s) spoken: Some English.
Facilities: Parking, TV room, meeting rooms, bar, chapel.
Season: Open all year.
DIRECTIONS:
Car: A1, exit Arezzo north to Bibbiera. Take local road east to La Verna.

San Gimignano

Convento Sant'Agostino
Piazza Sant'Agostino, 10
San Gimignano 53037 (Siena)
Tel. (0577) 940 383 ▪ Fax (0575) 940 383

This convent is part of a fifteenth-century complex on an old piazza in San Gimignano. Charming, comfortable rooms that offer wonderful views are available for visitors. The cloister is lovely and the adjacent Romanesque-Gothic Church of Sant'Agostino, dating from 1280, houses the finest art in the town—the beautiful frescoes of Benozzo Gozzoli depicting the life of Saint Augustine. The house is usually for groups, but call ahead to see if a room is available.

Rooms: 19 singles and doubles; none with bath.
Meals: Breakfast included.
Price: 30.000L per person.
Credit cards: Not accepted.
Curfew: Flexible.
Language(s) spoken: English.
Facilities: Parking, garden, chapel.
Season: Open all year.
DIRECTIONS:
Train station: Poggibonsi. Take local bus to San Gimignano.
Car: From the Super Strada between Florence and Siena, exit Poggibonsi and follow signs to San Gimignano (11 kilometers); take Porta San Matteo to Piazza Agostino.

Siena

Hotel Alma Domus
Via Camporegio, 37
Siena 53100 (Siena)
Tel. (0577) 441 77/444 87 ▪ Fax (0577) 476 01

A djacent to the beautiful sanctuary of Saint Catherine of Siena, Alma Domus is reached by ancient stone stairs that descend along a narrow alley. The hotel is entered through a pretty terrace adorned with plants, flowers and outdoor furniture. The main rooms are nice and roomy, the bedrooms are plain but comfortable and have modern baths; in some, french doors open on to little balconies with grand views of the city and duomo. This sight is even more spectacular at night, when the cathedral is brilliantly illuminated. One can explore all of Siena from here, but bring good walking shoes, as it is truly a hill town.

Rooms: 31 doubles and triples; most with bath.
Meals: Breakfast extra (9.000L).
Price: 75.000L (double); 105.000L (triple).
Credit cards: Not accepted.
Curfew: 11:30 P.M.
Language(s) spoken: Some English.
Facilities: TV room, chapel.
Season: Open all year.
DIRECTIONS:
Train/bus station: Florence. Take local bus to Siena. Walk to Via Camporegio; follow signs to Alma Domus.
Car: A1 (Florence/Siena), exit San Marco; follow "Centro" signs to Via Camporegio (near the bus station).

NOTES

UMBRIA

Lakes, rivers, mountains and rolling hills define the topography of this small region in the very center of Italy. Believed to be inhabited before the Etruscans arrived, the region fell victim to much the same fate as the rest of Italy as invader after invader conquered the land. By 1540, however, the region was a papal state and in 1860 became part of the Kingdom of Italy. Perugia, the capital, is a large, ancient hill town well known for its art, monuments, textiles and delicious chocolate candy.

Umbria's fairly prosperous economy is primarily based on agriculture and its chemical, steel, food and clothing industries. Regional crafts are handmade in clay, iron, wood and lace. Tourism in Umbria is far less developed than in nearby regions; nonetheless, it has much to offer with regard to interesting religious and historical sites and in art, music, food and wines. There are many convents in Umbria.

Assisi, a perfectly preserved hill town, is the crown jewel of Umbria. The birthplace of Saint Francis and Saint Clare, it is situated on the forested slopes of Mount Subasio, a walled city of steep, narrow streets and simple stone buildings that exudes a mystical serenity. Assisi offers something for all who come: for pilgrims, the peace and gentleness of the two saints can be experienced in all of the city's holy places. For art lovers, there is the first-century B.C. temple of Minerva that has been turned into a church located on the Piazza del Commune. Marvelous medieval masterpieces abound throughout the town, especially the famous frescoes of Giotto.

Potential visitors to the area should be aware that the October 1997 earthquake did a great deal of damage to Assisi. However, more harm was done to the art than the buildings. The upper Basilica of Saint Francis will be closed until the year 2000 to restore the building and the Giotto frescoes.

Close to Foligno and Assisi there is the small town of Bevagna.

The countryside is peaceful and beautiful, but the town itself is not especially interesting, with the exception of San Michele and San Silvestro, two Romanesque churches.

Foligno was bombed heavily in World War II; as a result, there is not much of historic interest in this sprawling Umbrian town. On the Rome/Ancona train line, Foligno is a common place to change trains; its proximity to Assisi and Spoleto makes it a convenient stopover, particularly if those towns are packed with tourists.

Dramatically perched high on a hill and visible for miles around, Orvieto is an ancient Etruscan hill town. The art and architecture, especially the magnificent duomo, are worthy of a visit; the town is also known for its lace, embroidery and fine white wines.

In a mountainous region of Umbria, Gubbio is a little medieval masterpiece of steep, narrow streets and well-preserved ancient monuments. Noted for its red-glazed pottery and local truffles, it has two grand folk festivals held every May.

A small town on the plains outside Assisi, Santa Maria degli Angeli, is important for its magnificent sixteenth-century basilica built around the Porziuncola, the place of Saint Francis's death.

A magical medieval hill town rising from the plains of Umbria, Todi is a delight of narrow streets, notable buildings and an exquisite piazza. Not yet overrun by hordes of tourists, it should be on the "to do" list.

Assisi

Casa del Terziario
Piazza del Vescovado, 5
Assisi 06081 (Perugia)
Tel. (075) 812 366 ▪ Fax (075) 816 377

A noble family of Assisi once inhabited this sixteenth-century palazzo. Today, gracious nuns welcome visitors to their home on the Piazza Vescovado, a small public plaza where Saint Francis returned all his worldly goods and garments to his father and began his new life of prayer and ministry. The sisters have fine accommodations, many with balconies and views, a small cloistered flower garden, a beautiful chapel and a rooftop terrace offering an incredible panorama of Assisi and the Umbrian countryside.

Rooms: Singles, doubles and triples; most with bath.
Meals: Breakfast included; half and full board available upon request.
Price: 44.000L–49.000L per person.
Credit cards: Not accepted.
Curfew: Flexible.
Language(s) spoken: English.
Facilities: Parking, elevator, library, chapel.
Season: April 1–October 31.
DIRECTIONS:
Train station: Santa Maria degli Angeli (on the Foligno-Terontola line). Take a taxi or local bus (every 30 minutes) to Piazza del Commune.
Car: SS 75, follow signs to Assisi. There is some parking here, so call for directions.

Casa di Santa Brigida
Via Moiano, 1
Assisi 06081 (Perugia)
Tel. (075) 812 693 ■ Fax (075) 813 216

Tucked into a gentle slope just outside Assisi's medieval walls, the Brigittines welcome visitors to their lovely Umbrian house. The garden and terrace are wonderful for relaxation; the accommodations are immaculate and simple, some with views of Assisi's red-tiled roofs and the Basilica of Saint Francis, while others offer Umbrian country vistas. The public rooms are nicely furnished and an excellent library is open to all. A five-minute climb up a narrow stone path leads to the historical center.

Rooms: 19 singles and doubles; all with bath.
Meals: Breakfast included; half and full board available upon request.
Price: 65.000L (single); 70.000L–90.000L (double).
Credit cards: Not accepted.
Curfew: None.
Language(s) spoken: English.
Facilities: Parking, elevator, TV room, meeting room, library, chapel.
Season: Open all year.
DIRECTIONS:
Train station: Santa Maria degli Angeli. Take bus (every 30 minutes) and ask driver to stop at the house.
Car: SS 75 and follow signs to Assisi. The house is on the left, shortly after you turn on to V. Vittorio Emanuele. It comes up quickly, so be on the lookout.

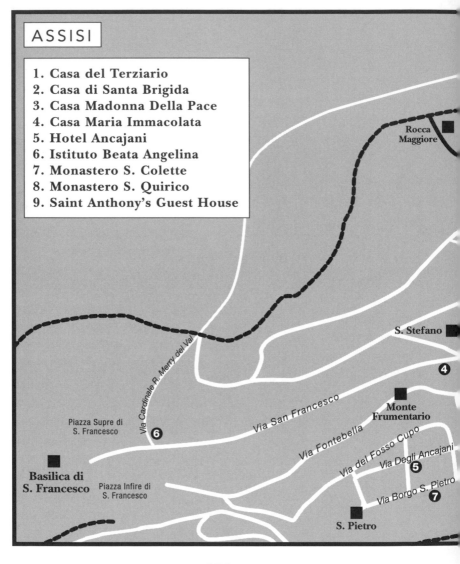

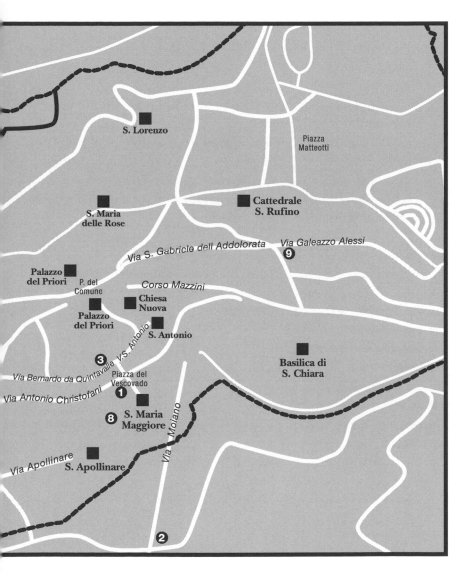

S. Lorenzo

Piazza
Matteotti

S. Maria
delle Rose

Cattedrale
S. Rufino

Via S. Gabriele dell Addolorata

Via Galeazzo Alessi

❾

Palazzo
del Priori

P. del
Comune

Corso Mazzini

Chiesa
Nuova

Palazzo
del Priori

V. S. Antonio

S. Antonio

❸

Basilica di
S. Chiara

Via Bernardo da Quintavalle

Piazza del
Vescovado

Via Antonio Christofani

❶

❽

S. Maria
Maggiore

Via Moiano

Via Apollinare

S. Apollinare

❷

Casa Madonna Della Pace
Via Bernardo da Quintavalle, 16
Assisi 06081 (Perugia)
Tel. (075) 812 337 ■ Fax (075) 816 851

Near the center of medieval Assisi, this unobtrusive stone house has extraordinarily beautiful frescoes adorning the ceilings of several of its main rooms. Some of the bedrooms offer great comfort in exquisite, hand-carved, antique beds. A pretty chapel, meeting room and quiet garden are available for guests. The sisters are extremely hospitable and very organized; they cater mainly to groups, but will take individuals if there is space.

Rooms: Singles, doubles and triples; most with bath.
Meals: Breakfast included; half and full board available upon request.
Price: 40.000L per person.
Credit cards: Not accepted.
Curfew: 10:00 P.M.
Laguage(s) spoken: No English.
Facilities: Elevator, library, chapel.
Season: Open all year.
DIRECTIONS:
Train station: Santa Maria degli Angeli. Take local bus to Piazza del Carmine.
Car: SS 75, follow signs to Assisi and head for "Centro."

Casa Maria Immacolata

Via San Francesco, 13

Assisi 06081 (Perugia)

Tel. (075) 812 267 ▪ Fax (075) 816 258

Terra-cotta pots overflowing with colorful flowers are attached to the Umbrian stone walls of this special house. Entering through an arched doorway, one is warmly greeted by the sisters, who delight in showing their home to visitors. They have a fine TV room with a balcony that reveals a memorable and breathtaking panorama of the valley below; prettily decorated bedrooms offer the same view (odd numbered rooms) and there is a magnificent, tiny chapel that is also accessible to the street. Along the same street is a small, vaulted workshop occupied by a local craftsman who carves the crosses of Saint Francis in the same manner as has been done for centuries.

Rooms: Singles, doubles and triples; all with bath.
Meals: Breakfast included; half and full board available upon request.
Price: 40.000L per person.
Credit cards: Not accepted.
Curfew: 10:00 P.M.
Language(s) spoken: English, some French.
Facilities: Chapel.
Season: Open March–November.
DIRECTIONS:
Train station: Santa Maria degli Angeli. Take local bus to Piazza del Comune.

Hotel Ancajani

Via Ancajani, 16

Assisi 06081 (Perugia)

Tel. (075) 815 128 ▪ Fax (075) 815 129

Situated about two hundred yards from the magnificent Basilica of Saint Francis, this two-star hotel was completely restored in 1993. The sisters offer good food, nice accommodations and pleasant surroundings. It is a very convenient base for visiting this medieval town and not too far from the bustling town center, Piazza del Comune.

Rooms: 24 singles, doubles and triples; all with bath and telephone.
Meals: Breakfast extra (10.000L); full board available upon request.
Price: 75.000L (single); 90.000L (double).
Credit cards: Not accepted.
Curfew: Flexible.
Language(s) spoken: Some English, French.
Facilities: Elevator, meeting room, chapel.
Season: Open all year except January 10–February 10.
DIRECTIONS:
Train station: Santa Maria degli Angeli. Take local bus to Pizza. S. Pietro.
Car: SS 75 to Assisi.

Istituto Beata Angelina
Via Merry del Val, 4
Assisi 06081 (Perugia)
Tel. (075) 812 511 ▪ Fax (075) 812 511

D irectly across from the Basilica of Saint Francis, Franciscan sisters direct this lovely stone guesthouse. One enters through a beautiful flower-filled gravel courtyard that has benches, tables and chairs for guests' rest and relaxation. Accommodations are good, and many of the rooms have spectacular views of the basilica and plains below. Close to restaurants and shops, it is in a busy section of Assisi. Most visitors come in organized groups, but if the sisters have room, they will take individuals.

Rooms: 18 singles, doubles and triples; most with bath.
Meals: Breakfast included; half and full board available upon request.
Price: 45.000L per person.
Credit cards: Not accepted.
Curfew: Flexible.
Language(s) spoken: French, German.
Facilities: Elevator, meeting room, chapel. Season: March–October.
DIRECTIONS:
Train station: Santa Maria degli Angeli. Take bus B to stop no. 9.
Car: SS 75 to Assisi.

Monastero S. Colette

Borgo San Pietro, 3

Assisi 06081 (Perugia)

Tel. (075) 812 345 ▪ Fax (075) 816 489

R eached through a covered walkway, this early-twentieth-century monastery is in a wonderful location, very near to the Basilica of Saint Francis. Directed by efficient French sisters, it is a pretty house with lovely antique-filled public rooms and comfortable accommodations. The sisters do not serve lunch or dinner but will suggest restaurants and even prepare picnics, which would be fun to take on a walk or a drive into the picturesque Umbrian countryside.

Rooms: Singles, doubles and triples; most with bath.
Meals: None, but picnics can be prepared if notice is given the night before.
Price: 40.000L per person.
Credit cards: Not accepted.
Curfew: None.
Language(s) spoken: English, French, some German.
Facilities: Parking, TV room, chapel.
Season: April 15–October 15.
DIRECTIONS:
Train station: Santa Maria degli Angeli. Take local bus to Piazza San Pietro.
Car: SS 75 to Assisi. The sisters have parking and will give you directions when you make reservations.

Monastero S. Quirico
Via Giovanni di Bonino
Assisi 06081 (Perugia)
Tel. (075) 812 688

Midway between the Basilicas of Saint Francis and Saint Clare, a small white stone guesthouse is available for pilgrims and tourists. Beyond the walled entrance, a flight of many stairs leads to the front door. The accommodations and public rooms are simple, clean and comfortable. The location is close to historic holy sites, restaurants and shops.

Rooms: 14 singles, doubles and triples; most with bath.
Meals: Breakfast included; half and full board available.
Price: 30.000L–35.000L per person.
Credit cards: Not accepted.
Curfew: 10:00 P.M.
Language(s) spoken: No English.
Facilities: Chapel.
Season: April 1–October 31.
DIRECTIONS:
Train station: Santa Maria degli Angeli, take a local bus or a taxi.

Saint Anthony's Guest House

Via G. Alessi, 10

Assisi 06081 (Perugia)

Tel. (075) 812 542 ▪ Fax (075) 813 723

A twelfth-century vaulted stone dining room is only one of the highlights of this wonderful home that has welcomed visitors to Assisi for more than sixty years. Directed by an American order from New York, it offers gracious hospitality in a sparkling clean house that provides panoramic views from the pretty upper garden, the library, sitting room and a few of the bedrooms, some of which have tiny balconies. Hopefully, Sister Marge, an American artist and nun, will be there to greet you when you visit this special guesthouse in the birthplace of Saint Francis.

Rooms: Singles, doubles and triples; all with bath.
Meals: Breakfast included; half and full board available upon request.
Price: 42.000L (single); 72.000L (double); 105.000L (triple).
Credit cards: Not accepted.
Curfew: Flexible.
Language(s) spoken: English.
Facilities: Parking (extra), elevator, TV room, conference facilities, library, chapel.
Season: Open Spring, closed Winter.
DIRECTIONS:
Train station: Santa Maria degli Angeli. Take local bus to Piazza del Comune or Piazza Matteotti
Car: SS 75, follow signs to Assisi. The sisters have limited parking; ask for directions when making reservations.

Bevagna

Casa Religiosa di Ospitalita

Corso Matteotti, 15

Bevagna 06031 (Perugia)

Tel. (0742) 360 133 ▪ Fax (0742) 360 135

Situated in the ancient Umbrian town of Bevagna, which Saint Francis often visited, the Benedictines offer hospitality and Italian language classes (for those who wish to study). The rooms are clean and modest in this centuries-old monastery, which has a very attractive cloistered courtyard encircling an ancient well. Olive oil, wine, marmalade and other products produced by the monks are sold on the premises.

Rooms: 52 singles, doubles and triples; all with bath.
Meals: Breakfast included; half and full board available upon request.
Price: 45.000L per person.
Credit cards: Not accepted.
Curfew: Flexible.
Language(s) spoken: Some English.
Facilities: Parking, elevator, meeting rooms, chapel.
Season: Open all year.
DIRECTIONS:
Train station: Foligno. Take a taxi; approximately 9 kilometers.
Car: From SS 75 (between Perugia and Foligno), take SS 316 to Bevagna.

Foligno

Oasi S. Francesco
Colle Cappuccini
Foligno 06034 (Perugia)
Tel. (0742) 350 262 ▪ Fax (0742) 340 854

Perched on a slope in the lush Umbrian hills, this modern structure was built in 1961 and remodeled in 1996. Run by Cappucine friars, hospitality is available for both vacations and retreats. Beautiful gardens, nice public rooms and simple accommodations overlooking vineyards and olive groves are but a few features of this sprawling complex. The captivating hill towns of Perugia and Assisi are nearby.

Rooms: Singles, doubles and triples; all with bath.
Meals: Breakfast included; half and full board available upon request.
Price: 35.000L per person.
Credit cards: Not accepted.
Curfew: No.
Language(s) spoken: No English.
Facilities: TV room, meeting rooms, parking, chapel.
Season: Open March–November.
DIRECTIONS:
Train station: Foligno. Take a taxi (approximately 3 kilometers).
Car: From SS 75 (Perugia-Foligno), watch for signs.

Gubbio

Hotel Beniamino Ubaldi
Via Perugina, 74
Gubbio 06024 (Perugia)
Tel. (075) 927 7773 ▪ Fax (075) 927 6604

Just outside the entrance to the walled, medieval city of Gubbio, this lovely three-star hotel owned by the local diocese welcomes tourists and retreatants alike. The main-floor rooms are extremely attractive, with cozy sitting areas and an abundance of fresh flowers. The bedrooms are pretty, with many amenities, including servi-bars. Surrounded by a park, the hotel is within easy walking distance of an elegant seventeenth-century baroque church, a first-century Roman theater and the historical, charming town itself.

Rooms: 62 singles and doubles; all with bath, telephone, TV and servi-bar.
Meals: Breakfast included; half and full board available upon request.
Price: 75.000L–100.000L (single); 95.000L–120.000L (double).
Credit cards: All major.
Curfew: No.
Language(s) spoken: Some English.
Facilities: Parking, elevator, conference facilities, restaurant, bar, gym, chapel.
Season: Open all year.
DIRECTIONS:
Train station: Fossato di Vico (on Rome-Ancona line). Transfer to a local bus (Gubbio is about 7 kilometers).
Car: From Perugia take SS 298. The hotel is on the left, just before the walled city.

Istituto Maestre Pie Filippine
Corso Garibaldi, 100
Gubbio 06024 (Perugia)
Tel. (075) 927 3768

L ocated along one of the principal pedestrian walkways in this
ancient town of narrow, steep, cobblestone streets is a small, old
guesthouse. Behind impressive wooden doors, a large stone foyer
opens onto a pretty flowered garden; to the left a narrow hall leads
to formal public rooms. Upstairs, the accommodations are plain yet
adequate. The location is grand for exploring the many churches,
palazzi and ceramic shops in this fascinating and well-preserved
medieval town famous for its pottery and truffles.

Rooms: 6 singles and doubles; all with bath.
Meals: Breakfast included.
Price: 30.000L per person.
Credit cards: Not accepted.
Curfew: Flexible.
Language(s) spoken: No English.
Facilities: Elevator, TV room, chapel.
Season: Open all year.
DIRECTIONS:
Train station: Fossato di Vico (on Rome-Ancona line). Take local
bus (approximately 7 kilometers).
Car: From Perugia, take SS 298. Pay-parking is available outside the
walled city.

Orvieto

Istituto Santissimo Salvatore
Via del Popolo, 1
Orvieto 05018 (Terni)
Tel. (0763) 342 910 ▪ Fax (0763) 342 910

Steps away from the bustling Piazza del Popolo, Dominican sisters run a nice guesthouse in this wonderful medieval town. The drab building belies the convenience, comfort and hospitality found within. Just a short walk away is the famous thirteenth-century Gothic cathedral built to honor the miracle of Bolsena; the facade of this duomo is one of the most magnificent in Europe, and the interior houses the relics of the miracle as well as beautiful Fra Angelico frescoes. The town is filled with quaint shops and restaurants that sell the fine white wines for which Orvieto is famous.

Rooms: 14 singles and doubles; all with bath.
Meals: Breakfast included; half and full board available upon request.
Price: 50.000L (single); 80.000L (double).
Credit cards: Not accepted.
Curfew: 10:30 P.M.
Language(s) spoken: No English.
Facilities: Parking, elevator, meeting room, library, chapel.
Season: Open all year.
DIRECTIONS:
Train station: Orvieto. Take local shuttle to Piazza Duomo; walk NW to Piazza del Popolo.
Car: A1, exit Orvieto and follow signs to "Centro" (there is pay-parking in the old town).

Santa Maria degli Angeli

Domus Pacis

Piazza Porziuncola, 1

Santa Maria degli Angeli 06088 (Perugia)

Tel. (075) 804 3530 ▪ Fax (075) 804 0455

Built in 1950 and designated a two-star hotel, this large institutional facility is operated by the Franciscans for both visiting groups and individuals. It has clean, simple bedrooms, a modern chapel and several meeting rooms, some of which are equipped with facilities for simultaneous translation in six languages. Across the plaza in front of the hotel is the magnificent baroque Basilica of Santa Maria degli Angeli, which houses the tiny Porziuncola in which Saint Francis started his order of friars and where he died in 1226.

Rooms: 84 singles, doubles and triples; all with bath and telephone.
Meals: Breakfast included; half and full board available upon request.
Price: 45.000L–65.000L (single); 70.000L–85.000L (double).
Credit cards: Not accepted.
Curfew: Flexible.
Language(s) spoken: English.
Facilities: Parking, elevator, TV room, many meeting rooms, restaurant, bar, chapel.
Season: Open all year.
DIRECTIONS:
Train station: Santa Maria degli Angeli. Walk to hotel (approximately two blocks).
Car: SS 75 (Perugia-Foligno), follow signs to Santa Maria degli Angeli. The hotel is on the right in the middle of the town.

Hotel Cenacolo Francescano
Viale Patrono d'Italia, 70
Santa Maria degli Angeli 06088 (Perugia)
Tel. (075) 804 1083 ▪ Fax (075) 804 0552

On the narrow road leading into Assisi this large two-star hotel is an option if the ancient hill town is full. The Umbrian stone structure is built around a cloistered courtyard sprinkled with benches on grassy areas. The accommodations are sparse, but some of the rooms have nice views of the countryside. There is a grand chapel, a spacious common room, an enormous dining room upstairs for groups and a small, drab dining room off the courtyard that is reserved for individual travelers. Unless the friars are present, our experience was that hospitality and efficiency are sadly lacking.

Rooms: 144 singles, doubles and triples; all with bath and telephone.
Meals: Breakfast included; half and full board available upon request.
Price: 43.000L–63.000L (single); 65.000L–85.000L (double).
Credit cards: Not accepted.
Curfew: Flexible.
Language(s) spoken: Some English.
Facilities: Parking, elevator, TV room, meeting rooms, bar, chapel.
Season: Open all year.
DIRECTIONS:
Train station: Santa Maria degli Angeli. Take a taxi or local bus.
Car: SS 75 (Perugia-Foligno), follow signs toward Assisi. The hotel is on the right immediately after going through Santa Maria degli Angeli.

Todi

Pensionato Santissima Annunziata
Via San Biagio, 2
Todi 06059 (Perugia)
Tel. (075) 894 2268 ▪ Fax (075) 894 2268

Set back from the ancient street is a beautiful wooden doorway flanked by large terra-cotta pots of bright blossoms. Inside is an exquisite convent that is an antique dealer's dream. It is more like a museum with elegant antique furniture, marble floors and walls adorned with ecclesiastical oil paintings. A grand chandelier and spectacular frescoes decorate the ceiling of the main reception room, and french doors open on to a wonderful garden. A few minutes' walk up the narrow, winding street will bring you to the lovely medieval piazza of this tiny, magical village.

Rooms: 34 singles, doubles and triples; all with bath.
Meals: Breakfast included; half and full board available upon request.
Price: 45.000L per person.
Credit cards: Not accepted.
Curfew: 10:30 P.M.
Language(s) spoken: French, German.
Facilities: Elevator, meeting room, chapel.
Season: Open all year.
DIRECTIONS:
Train station: Perugia. Take a bus to Porte Perugina (Todi), and walk up V. di Borgo Nuovo to V. S. Biagio (it is several steep blocks).
Car: A1 to SS 448 (south of Orvieto), exit Todi, follow signs to "Centro." The streets are incredibly old and narrow; driving is very, very difficult.

VALLE D'AOSTA

In the shadows of the magnificent Matterhorn and equally majestic Mount Blanc, Valle d' Aosta is an absolute delight of glorious peaks and valleys. The history of the region dates back to 24 B.C., when Roman conquerors founded the capital city, Aosta. Remarkable ruins from that period still exist: town walls, the Porta Praetoria and amphitheater among them. After the Romans came the Goths, Lombards and Franks until the eleventh century, when the Savoy family took control and ruled almost continuously for the next several centuries. In 1948, the region became semiautonomous.

Today, as in the past, the area is a major crossroads between Italy, France and Switzerland. The only difference is that one can travel by car through the incredible mountain tunnels or take a fantastic funicular journey and float over the summit of Mount Blanc between Courmayer and Chamonix instead of traversing the awesome Alps on foot.

Presently, tourism is the main industry; the region's geography pretty much determines that fact. Skiing and winter sports are available in fancy Courmayer as well as many villages and hamlets around the mountains. The forests and lake areas provide wonderful hiking adventures, and a huge portion of the region has been preserved in the spectacular Gran Paradiso National Park. The economy is also enhanced by the crafts industry, which produces lovely carved wooden and wrought iron objects. A fair amount of good regional cheese and wine is also sold.

Saint-Oyen is a tiny alpine hamlet on the road to Switzerland. The surrounding area is rural, and the town has a few cute shops and restaurants plus a small tennis complex. The little village is a good stopping point for those who wish to visit the Great Saint Bernard Hospice and see the famous rescue dogs. The puppies are usually "in residence" from the end of May to mid-September.

Saint-Oyen

Casa Ospitaliera del Gran San Bernardo
Via Flassin, 1
Saint-Oyen 11010 (Aosta)
Tel. (0165) 782 47

For centuries the hospitality of the Saint Bernard monks has been renowned. Today that tradition continues in a delightful casa nestled on the meadowed slopes of the Italian Alps. The house sits just yards away from the road that travelers and conquerors have used to cross these majestic mountains since 800 B.C. The building is fairly new, built as an alpine monastery fashioned with foot-thick whitewashed walls, flagstone floors and incredible furniture, all handcrafted by the monks. Most of the rooms are wood-paneled with hand-carved beds; bathrooms are modern and sparkling clean. This is a wonderful stop for those crossing the Alps or adventurers who wish to ski, hike or journey to the pass to see the famous Saint Bernard dogs.

Rooms: Singles, doubles and triples; some with bath.
Meals: Full board only.
Price: 50.000L per person (with full board).
Credit cards: Not accepted.
Curfew: Flexible.
Language(s) spoken: No English.
Facilities: Parking, elevator, meeting rooms, library, chapel.
Season: Open all year except May.
DIRECTIONS:
Train Station: Aosta. Take bus from Piazza Narbonne to Saint-Oyen.
Car: From Aosta north (highway number 27) to Saint-Oyen.

NOTES

VENETO

Bordered on the north by Austria and on the east by the Adriatic Sea, Veneto's topography includes mountains (Alps and Dolomites), part of the Po Valley, and the Venetian plain. Romans, Huns, Lombards and Byzantines have marched through this glorious region until its jewel, Venice, became a maritime superpower, bringing stability, wealth and glory to all of Veneto. The Renaissance flourished here as evidenced by the incredible art and architecture in the area. In 1860, Veneto became part of the Kingdom of Italy.

Most of the region enjoys a good, healthy economy based on industries of all size: textiles, shoes, furniture, ceramics and fishing. Small craft businesses in jewelry, glass, ceramics, furniture and lace are quite prevalent, and tourism thrives. There are convents available in many parts of Veneto.

In the Dolomites, Borca di Cadore is a small town of steepled churches, little shops and alpine restaurants located in a rural mountain area on the scenic road to Cortina.

Cortina D'Ampezzo, a sparkling gem, is in the heart of the Dolomites. Encircled by mountains and meadows, it pulsates with life around the clock regardless of season. Home of the 1956 winter Olympics, it offers world-class winter and summer activities, elegant shops, excellent restaurants and incomparable scenery.

Pieve di Cadore is a small, charming town nestled against the Dolomites. A small lively piazza in the old "Centro" is sprinkled with busy cafes, and the family-friendly citizens have built an adorable Santa Claus House for children in the public park.

On the plains of Veneto, Monteortone is on the outskirts of Padua. This small spa town in a residential area is blessed with the same beautiful setting as the more glitzy Abano Terme, which is adjacent. For rest, relaxation and enjoying "the waters," this is a good choice.

Heavily bombed during World War II, Padua lost many of its treasures; enough enticements remain, however, to warrant a visit. These include the small medieval center, Scrovegni Chapel, the ancient university of Dante and Galileo and the Basilica of Saint Anthony, the final resting place of the famous Franciscan friar.

Venice is a must. A magical city of canals and gondolas, elegant palazzi and simple dwellings, superb art and grand architecture, fancy boutiques and lively markets, fine restaurants and neighborhood cafes, glorious opera and singing gondoliers—for young and old, it is a fantasy come true!

Borca di Cadore

Dolomiti Pio X
Via Roma, 71
Borca di Cadore 32040 (Belluno)
Tel. (0436) 890 356 ▪ Fax (0436) 9408

Built early in the twentieth century, this distinguished gray stone structure was originally the "Palace Hotel of the Dolomites." The belle epoque style of the public rooms is truly grand, with elegant wood floors, old oriental carpets, antique furniture and beautiful crystal chandeliers. Many of the bedrooms are filled with the original furnishings. The house and terraces are surrounded by the majestic Dolomites. During the school year part of the building is a small school run by the diocesan priests, but guests are warmly welcomed year-round.

Rooms: Singles and doubles; all with bath and telephone.
Meals: Full board only.
Price: 62.000L–83.000L per person.
Credit cards: Not accepted.
Curfew: No.
Language(s) spoken: Some English.
Facilities: Parking, elevator, TV room, conference facilities, library, restaurant, bar, tennis, chapel.
Season: Open all year.
DIRECTIONS:
Car: Take SS 51 north from Belluno. The hotel is on the left just outside of Borca di Cadore.

Cortina

Soggiorno Missionarie dell' Eucaristia
Via 29 Maggio, 4
Cortina 32043 (Belluno)
Tel. (0436) 4662 ▪ Fax (0436) 863 817

A small doorway and a narrow flight of stairs leads to the interior of this charming guesthouse. The sisters have furnished the knotty-pine rooms with antiques and plant-filled copper pots. These alpine accommodations are cozy, and several rooms have balconies overlooking the campanile and the pedestrian zone, which is brimming with elegant, expensive shops and wonderful restaurants serving delectable food. Magnificent views of the surrounding Dolomites are to be had from this ski town that "buzzes" nearly year-round.

Rooms: Singles and doubles; all with bath.
Meals: Breakfast included.
Price: 95.000L–110.000L per person.
Credit cards: Not accepted.
Curfew: No.
Language(s) spoken: No English.
Facilities: TV room, chapel.
Season: Open all year.
DIRECTIONS:
Train station: Calalzo di Cadore. Take the local bus for Cortina.
Car: Take SS 51 north of Belluno, follow signs to Cortina and head toward "Centro" to Via Marconi, then turn left on 29 Maggio.

Monteortone

Albergo Terme Mamma Margherita
Via Monteortone, 63
Monteortone 35030 (Padova)
Tel. (049) 866 9350 ▪ Fax (049) 866 9041

I n a good residential area on the outskirts of this famous spa town, Abano Terme, Mamma Margherita is operated under the direction of the Salesians of Don Bosco. Set in a pretty park of tall fir trees and rolling lawns, a rather uninteresting exterior hides a facility with simple rooms, nice, large public areas and complete spa services, including mineral water and mud baths. Behind the hotel, tables and chairs are set on the lawn leading to a fancy glass-enclosed swimming pool.

Rooms: 95 singles and doubles; all with bath.
Meals: Breakfast included.
Price: 72.000L–80.000L per room.
Credit cards: Not accepted.
Curfew: No.
Language(s) spoken: No English.
Facilities: Parking, elevator, TV room, library, bar, spa facilities, swimming pool, chapel.
Season: Open mid-March–mid-November.
DIRECTIONS:
Train station: Padua. Take local bus A or AT and stop at Mamma Margherita.
Car: From A13 or A4, follow signs to Abano Terme. Continue to Monteortone and watch for the hotel signs.

Albergo Terme San Marco
Via Santuario, 130
Monteortone 35030 (Padova)
Tel. (049) 866 9041 ▪ Fax (049) 667 286

In 1450 this beautifully restored building was a convent. Set in a large park, the facade is a fascinating design of light and dark stone. Inside, the public rooms and many of the bedrooms have tiled floors and coved ceilings. The house is built around a cloistered courtyard of manicured lawns, floral gardens and an ancient well. Sometimes during the summer there is evening entertainment in this picturesque setting. The spa and recreation facilities of the adjacent hotel are open to guests of San Marco.

Rooms: 50 singles and doubles; all with bath.
Meals: Breakfast included.
Price: 68.000L–77.000L (per room).
Credit cards: Not accepted.
Curfew: No.
Language(s) spoken: Some English.
Facilities: Parking, elevator, TV room, library, bar, chapel.
Season: Open all year.
DIRECTIONS:
Train station: Padua. Take local bus A or AT to Mamma Margherita.
Car: A13 or A4, follow signs to Abano Terme and continue to Monteortone. Watch for hotel signs.

Padua

Casa del Pellegrino
Via Cesarotti, 21
Padua 35123 (Padova)
Tel. (049) 875 2100 ▪ Fax (049) 875 3824

In 1775 the Hapsburg emperor Joseph II stayed in this hotel with family and friends. Today it has been modernized to such an extent that the original grandeur is sadly gone. Nonetheless, it is plain, clean and comfortable, with many rooms facing a quiet courtyard. Across the road from the Basilica of Saint Anthony, it is also convenient for visiting other historic sections of this city, including its ancient university, founded in 1222, making it one of the oldest universities in the world.

Rooms: Singles and doubles; most with bath.
Meals: Breakfast extra (8.000L); half and full board available upon request.
Price: 43.000L–72.000L (single); 60.000L–92.000L (double), depending on time of year and number of meals taken.
Credit cards: Most major.
Curfew: Flexible.
Language(s) spoken: Some English.
Facilities: Parking, elevator, TV room, conference facilities, restaurant, bar, chapel.
Season: Open February 8–December 15.
DIRECTIONS:
Train station: Padua. Take bus no. 8 to the Basilica of Saint Anthony.
Car: On reaching Padua, follow the yellow road signs for the Basilica of Saint Anthony.

Collegio Universitario Antonianum
Via Donatello, 24
Padua 35123 (Padova)
Tel. (049) 651 444 ▪ Fax (049) 654 966

Adjacent to Padua's pretty botanical gardens, the Antonianum is an excellent choice for a summer visit. The accommodations are plain and clean in this large, stone building, and there is a nice, quiet garden in the back. Located in a bustling area of Padua, it is a brief walk to the thirteenth-century Basilica of Saint Anthony (where he is buried) and an easy bus ride to the old city and its numerous art masterpieces, including Giotto's incredibly beautiful frescos in the Scrovegni Chapel.

Rooms: Singles, doubles and triples; none with bath.
Meals: Breakfast included; half and full board available upon request.
Price: 25.000L per person; 38.000L (half board); 53.000L (full board).
Credit cards: Not accepted.
Curfew: No.
Language(s) spoken: Some English.
Facilities: Elevator, TV room, billiard room, conference facilities, library, bar, chapel.
Season: Open July 15–September 30.
DIRECTIONS:
Train station: Padua. Take bus no. 8 to the Basilica of Saint Anthony.
Car: Upon reaching Padua, follow yellow road signs to Basilica of Saint Anthony.

Pieve di Cadore

Albergo Dolomiti
Pieve di Cadore
Pieve di Cadore 32044 (Belluno)
Tel. (0435) 500 392/500 479

On the outskirts of a small, charming alpine village nestled in the spectacular Dolomites, this two-star hotel offers simple, clean accommodations and a relaxing atmosphere. Located in a park, the enormous alpine building contains many balconied rooms with good views of the rural countryside and awesome Dolomites. It is advisable to go by car, as public transportation is not convenient. The sisters are open only in the summer months for vacationers.

Rooms: Singles, doubles and triples; most with bath.
Meals: Breakfast included.
Price: 75.000L–95.000L per person.
Credit cards: Not accepted.
Curfew: Flexible.
Language(s) spoken: No English.
Facilities: Parking, chapel.
Season: Open June 25–August 31.
DIRECTIONS:
Car: SS 51; about 12 kilometers north of Belluno watch for signs to Pieve di Cadore. As you head into the little town, V. Dolomiti is on the left.

Venice

Casa Caburlotto
Santa Croce, 316–Fondamenta Rizzi
Venice 30125 (Venezia)
Tel. (041) 710 877 ▪ Fax (041) 710 875

Within walking distance of the train station, Casa Caburlotto is on a little canal near the commercial port of Venice. While the neighborhood is not particularly good, the convent's accommodations are safe, clean and simple, with a lovely garden brimming with flowers in the back. The sisters are extremely kind and hospitable.

Rooms: Singles, doubles and triples; most with bath.
Meals: Breakfast included.
Price: 50.000L per person.
Credit cards: Not accepted.
Curfew: 10:30 P.M.
Language(s) spoken: No English.
Facilities: Chapel.
Season: Open all year.
DIRECTIONS:
Train station: Santa Lucia. Cross the small bridge in front of the station, turn right, walk to Fondamenta Cosetti, turn left and continue walking past Piazzale Roma to Fondamenta Rizzi; turn right. The Church of S. M. Maggiore is on the same canal.

Bed and Blessings: Italy

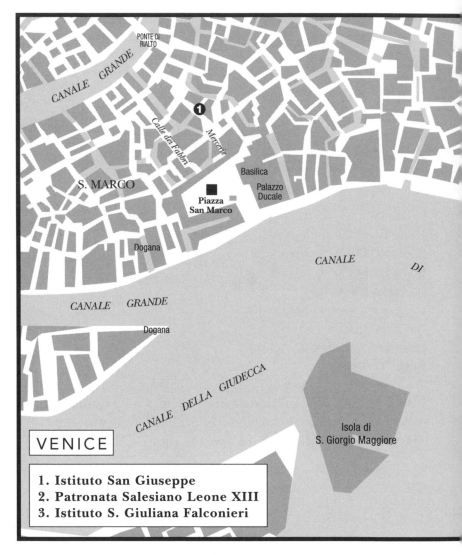

PONTE DI RIALTO

CANALE GRANDE

Calle dei Fabbri

Mercerie

1

S. MARCO

Basilica

Palazzo Ducale

Piazza San Marco

Dogana

CANALE GRANDE

Dogana

CANALE

DI

CANALE DELLA GIUDECCA

Isola di S. Giorgio Maggiore

VENICE

1. Istituto San Giuseppe
2. Patronata Salesiano Leone XIII
3. Istituto S. Giuliana Falconieri

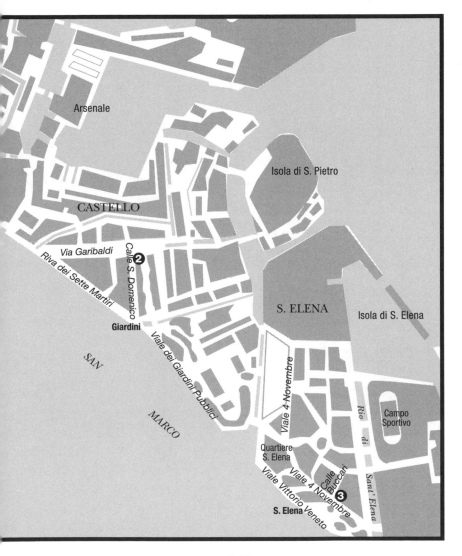

Casa Cardinal Piazza
Cannaregio 3539/A
Venice 30121 (Venezia)
Tel. (041) 721 388 ▪ Fax (041) 720 233

Two elegant gray palazzi, formerly occupied by noble Venetian families, are today known as Casa Cardinal Piazza. Located on a canal in the clean, quiet Cannaregio neighborhood, the casa offers gracious hospitality in plain, modern guest rooms and large public rooms. A garden is available for guests' enjoyment. Away from the hustle and bustle of San Marco, the casa is an easy walk or water bus ride to all the marvelous sights and sounds of Venice.

Rooms: 24 singles and doubles; all with bath.
Meals: Breakfast extra (5.000L); half and full board available upon request.
Price: 50.000L (single); 90.000L (double).
Credit cards: Not accepted.
Curfew: 11:00 P.M.
Language(s) spoken: Some English.
Facilities: Elevator, conference facilities, chapel.
Season: Open all year.
DIRECTIONS:
Train station: Santa Lucia. Take water bus no. 52, stopping at Madonna dell'Orto.

Istituto Artigianelli

Dorsoduro, 919

Venice 30123 (Venezia)

Tel. (041) 522 4077 ▪ Fax (041) 528 6214

Traveling by vaporetto up the undulating Giudecca Canal to the Zattere stop, one disembarks and steps just a few feet to the arched entrance of this stone guesthouse situated between a beautiful Jesuit church and the equally lovely fifteenth-century Church of Santa Maria della Visitazione. The accommodations are clean and simple, with a pretty cloistered garden in the center. Many students inhabit the Dorsoduro area, which accounts for the bustling atmosphere and busy cafes. The location is excellent for touring Venice by foot or boat.

Rooms: Singles and doubles; most with bath.
Meals: No meals.
Price: 70.000L (single); 110.000L(double).
Credit cards: Not accepted.
Curfew: 11:00 P.M.
Language(s) spoken: Some English.
Facilities: Elevator, TV room, library, chapel.
Season: Open all year.
DIRECTIONS:
Train station: Santa Lucia. Take water bus no. 52 to "Zattere" stop.

Istituto S. Giuliana Falconieri

Castello Calle Buccari, 10

Venice 30122 (Venezia)

Tel. (041) 522 0829 ▪ Fax (041) 520 5286

Run by kind, hospitable nuns, this guesthouse is a long walk from Piazza San Marco. The neighborhood and nearby park are very nice; however, the building is in only fair condition. The rooms are large, comfortable and clean; sitting areas are available for the guests, as is a pretty garden. During the academic year the sisters run a primary school; thus the house can be fairly noisy at times.

Rooms: Singles, doubles and triples; most with bath.
Meals: Breakfast included.
Price: 55.000L per person.
Credit cards: Not accepted.
Curfew: 10:30 P.M. (flexible).
Language(s) spoken: No English.
Facilities: Elevator, chapel.
Season: Open all year except August.
DIRECTIONS:
Train station: Santa Lucia. Take water bus no. 1 or no. 52 to S. Elina stop. Proceed through the park heading right to Calle Buccari.

Istituto San Giuseppe
Ponte della Guerra, Castello, 5402
Venice 30122 (Venezia)
Tel. (041) 522 5352 ▪ Fax (041) 522 4891

When you ring the doorbell at Istituto San Giuseppe, be sure to look at the amazing face carved around it! This is not the only surprise in this old, once elegant palazzo with its massive arched doorway flanked by stone Corinthian columns. Beyond the wooden doors are a flower-filled courtyard, modernized rooms and baths, and a small roof terrace from which one can observe the gondoliers and their colorful boats parked on the canal at the convent's entrance. In a superb location, Venice literally envelopes you with its sights, sounds and magic.

Rooms: 16 singles, doubles and triples; all with bath.
Meals: No meals.
Price: 60.000L–65.000L (single); 80.000L (double); 120.000L (triple).
Credit cards: Not accepted.
Curfew: 11:00 P.M.
Language(s) spoken: No English.
Facilities: Chapel.
Season: Open all year.
DIRECTIONS:
Train station: Santa Lucia. Take water bus no. 1 or no. 52 to Piazza San Marco. Cross the Piazza, walk two blocks on Mercerie and turn right; go about four blocks to Ponte Guerre (a bridge), cross it and turn left immediately.

Istituto Solesin
Dorsoduro, 624
Venice 30123 (Venezia)
Tel. (041) 522 4356 ▪ Fax (041) 523 8124

From the picturesque canal of San Vio, one ventures down a long, narrow walkway to Istituto Solesin. The sisters open this small, plain and quiet university pensione to travelers for only a few weeks in the summer. Located in a lovely area just off the Grand Canal, it is in a convenient spot for visiting the Accademia, the Guggenheim and the marvelous neighborhood art and craft galleries as well as the trendy shops and restaurants. You will feel more like a local than a tourist here.

Rooms: 11 singles, doubles and triples; all with bath.
Meals: Breakfast included.
Price: 50.000L per person.
Credit cards: Not accepted.
Curfew: 10:30 P.M.
Language(s) spoken: No English.
Facilities: Chapel.
Season: Open July 1–August 20.
DIRECTIONS:
Train station: Santa Lucia. Take water bus no. 12 to the "Accademia" stop.

Patronata Salesiano Leone XIII

Castelli, 1281 (Calle San Domenico)
Venice 30122 (Venezia)
Tel. 41 528 7299 ■ Fax 41 528 5189

Near beautiful public gardens in a modest Venetian neighborhood, the Salesians offer hospitality to summer visitors. The austere building is a university pensione during the academic year, and therefore the accommodations are quite simple, but certainly adequate for a short stay. One real benefit is the walk to San Marco along the canal bordered by shops, restaurants, cafes and hotels on one side and boats, gondolas and views of the Basilica of San Georgio Maggiore and Santa Maria della Salute on the other. It is a real treat for the eyes and ears!

Rooms: 31 singles and doubles; some with bath.
Meals: Breakfast included.
Price: 70.000L (single); 120.000L (double).
Credit cards: Not accepted.
Curfew: No.
Language(s) spoken: No English.
Facilities: Elevator, chapel.
Season: June 15–September 30.
DIRECTIONS:
Train station: Santa Lucia. Take water bus no. 52 to Giardini.

VENETO

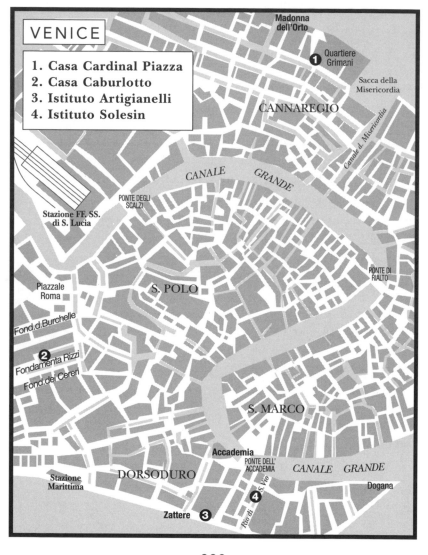

VENICE

1. Casa Cardinal Piazza
2. Casa Caburlotto
3. Istituto Artigianelli
4. Istituto Solesin

Madonna dell'Orto

Quartiere Grimani

Sacca della Misericordia

Canale d. Misericordia

CANNAREGIO

CANALE GRANDE

PONTE DEGLI SCALZI

Stazione FF. SS. di S. Lucia

PONTE DI RIALTO

Piazzale Roma

S. POLO

Fond.d.Burchelle

Fondamenta Rizzi

Fond.dei Cereri

S. MARCO

Accademia

PONTE DELL' ACCADEMIA

CANALE GRANDE

Stazione Marittima

DORSODURO

Rio di S. Vio

Dogana

Zattere

RESERVATION REQUEST

Convent Name _____

Address _____

Vorrei prenotare una stanza con il bagno   ☐
(Request for room with bath)

Vorrei prenotare una stanza senza bagno   ☐
(Request for room without bath)

Arrivo _____
(Arriving)

Partenza _____
(Departing)

Deposito incluso   ☐
(Deposit enclosed)

Grazie mille
(Thank you very much)

Sinceramente
(Sincerely)

RICHIESTA DI INFORMAZIONI
(RESERVATION INFORMATION)

Nome del Convento _____
(Name of Convent)

Indirizzo _____
(Address) _____

Prima di prenotare, desidererei ricevere le seguenti informazioni per
il periodo da_____ a _____.
(Before booking I would like to receive the following information for
the period from_____ to _____.)

Desponibilita' di:
(availability of)

STANZA (room)	PREZZO (cost)		PREZZO (cost)		PREZZO (cost)
signola (single) ____	_____	con bagno____ (with bath)	_____	con pasti ___ (with meals)	_____
doppia (double) ____	_____		_____		_____
tripla (triple) ____	_____		_____		_____

PASTI (meals)	colazione (breakfast) _____	pranzo (lunch) _____	cena (dinner) _____
DEPOSITO (deposit)	carta di credito (credit card) _____	assegno (check) _____	

Ringrazio della cortese attenzione e porgo cordiali saluti.
(Thank you. Sincerely)

_____

Si prega di rispedire al richiedente debitamente compilato.
(Please complete and return to sender.)